Contents

▼ ▼ ▼

Preface

▼ ▼ ▼

What an exciting time to be a stock investor! The stock market has performed marvelously over the past 15 years with no end in sight. The economy, with its current strong growth trend and low inflation, is in the best shape it has been in for years. Around the world, countries are rapidly moving toward democratic governments and free markets, the two most important underpinnings of economic prosperity. As a result, new stock markets are springing up everywhere enabling investors to share in this worldwide prosperity surge.

In this highly favorable environment, I hope you are already in the stock market or are about ready to jump in. For my part, I will do everything I can in *The Vest Pocket Guide to Value Investing* to make your investment in the stock market as profitable as possible. I will do my best to allay your concerns about putting your hard-earned money into a market that at times seems to march to the beat of a different drummer.

The Winning Value Investing Smorgasbord

The Vest Pocket Guide to Value Investing explores the full range of techniques that you will need to transform your individual stock decisions into a winning portfolio, everything from constructing your portfolio to doing economic and market analysis to valuing and selecting individual stocks. Along the way, I will make it easy for you to understand and then use a smorgasbord of value investing techniques.

Value investing revolves around the identification of undervalued stocks. Out of all the intellectual horsepower that has been focused on the stock market comes a very clear and simple message: *If you patiently apply the techniques of value investing, you can earn an above-average portfolio return*. In fact, it can mean hundreds of thousands of extra dollars in your portfolio at the end of your investment horizon.

The techniques of value investing are within everyone's reach. So why doesn't everyone use them? The key is patience. Value investing does not work all of the time, nor does it work with every stock. So you have to stick with value investing through thick and thin. Many investors are unwilling to wait out the dry spells. Like mutual fund managers and other professional investors, some are not in a position to be patient due to short-term profit pressures. So value investing is not suited for every investor. But it does work if you are willing to stick with it.

A Bit about Me

I have been teaching, researching and managing my own money for over 15 years. During this time, I have worked with many individual investors helping them construct and manage their stock portfolios. From these experiences, I am well aware of the practical problems facing investors when they try to implement value investing. I have also consulted with several large institutional investors, implementing some of the techniques that I describe in this book.

I have refined many of my ideas through my academic research at the Daniels College of Business at the University of Denver. This work has helped shape the set of practical value investing techniques presented in this book.

Over the last ten years, I have presented a stock analysis seminar for the American Association of Individual Investors (AAII) headquartered in Chicago, Illinois. About once a month I travel somewhere in the United States to present my ideas on how to create a winning stock portfolio. These experiences nationwide have proved to be an invaluable preparation for writing this book. AAII audiences demand clear and practical explanations of techniques that they can put to work immediately in their portfolios. The fact that I have survived for 10 years indicates that I have been able to meet these expectations.

Unlocking the Secrets of Value Investing

I suspect your expectations are not much different from those of my AAII audiences. So let's dive into the world of value investing. As your guide throughout this book, I have made every effort to make your journey a productive one. You will find a Value Investor's Checklist at the beginning of each chapter and dozens of Value Investor's Tips at the beginning of each subsection. These checklists and tips should allow you to quickly target the sections you want to read at the moment.

All the value investing techniques are applied to real companies so that you can better understand how to use them in your own situation. Because not everyone is comfortable working with numbers (a hard-learned lesson from years on the seminar circuit!), I present the techniques as straightforwardly as possible and keep the jargon to a minimum.

So let's get started!

Tom Howard
Denver, Colorado
June 1996

CHAPTER 1

▼ ▼ ▼

The Care and Feeding of Your Stock Portfolio

VALUE INVESTOR'S CHECKLIST

✓ Build your portfolio on a well-conceived master plan, resulting in a cross-section of stocks, industries and countries.

✓ Try to achieve an appropriate level of diversification even though it is difficult because it is natural for you to focus on those things you know best and thus produce a highly concentrated portfolio.

✓ Plan the proper level of activity to reap the benefits of value investing without making your broker rich.

✓ Measure your performance over time—an important aspect of managing your portfolio.

MAKING SOUND
PORTFOLIO DECISIONS

VALUE INVESTING TIPS

▼ Move beyond what is familiar to you to achieve proper portfolio construction.

▼ Take steps to ensure that your portfolio remains properly diversified through time.

▼ See a stock portfolio for what it is, a way to produce substantial wealth over time and not as a surrogate set of friends.

▼ Remain loyal to a stock only as long as it represents a value to you; if it isn't a value, get rid of it!

The thrill of analyzing and identifying high potential stocks attracts most serious investors to the stock market. *Value investing*, the major focus of this book, is the process of identifying undervalued and overvalued stocks in order to earn above-average returns. But before beginning the detailed work of value investing, a savvy investor will spend time considering the overall structure of the portfolio.

You might wonder why this is necessary. After all, you are on the path to becoming a value investor and value investing, if pursued faithfully, will produce superior returns. So why not just pick a bunch of value stocks and watch the returns roll in? This approach might work if it weren't for the natural but undesirable investing tendencies that you as an investor need to be aware of.

The Problem of Sticking with the Familiar

Many of us, in making any type of decision, tend to stick with what we know. In making daily purchasing decisions, you and I often ask trusted friends and relatives what brand to buy or what service to hire. You might even ask fellow workers how they make their financial decisions. You may find it hard to expand your personal horizon to the unknown because you might fear making a costly mistake. Thus a portfolio often reflects the investor's known world, such as a large concentration in your company's stock or in the stock of a family business. You might have just a few stocks, perhaps recommended by a friend or a relative. In other words, your portfolio is poorly diversified because of the purely natural tendency of staying with what is familiar.

The problem with such a concentrated portfolio is that on a risk and return basis it will perform poorly. That is, given the risk you have taken on, you will not produce, on average, a very attractive return. So a properly diversified portfolio is a must. We will look at the details of how to properly diversify in the next few sections. Your first step is to fight your natural tendency to stick with what is familiar.

Unconcentrating Your Portfolio

What if your portfolio is already highly concentrated, perhaps because you followed the advice of coworkers, family members or friends? This is one of the most difficult issues any investor faces. By trimming your current positions and investing in different stocks, you may feel like a traitor. You may feel like you are turning your back on an important part of your life and placing your hard-earned money with a group of strangers. This feeling may be particularly strong when those stocks have produced very good returns over the years. They almost seem like a part of the family! How could you get rid of such a close family member?

The tax laws provide a further hindrance to unconcentrating your portfolio. If the stock has risen dramatically over the years, then selling it may trigger a large capital gains tax. Because most of us don't like to pay taxes, we leave the portfolio highly concentrated. Why incur the certain tax bill for the seemingly nebulous benefits of diversifying? (As we will see in the next section, diversification benefits are real and significant.)

So how do you tackle this difficult problem? I think the best solution is to sell a portion of the portfolio each year. For example, you might decide to sell a third of each large stock position each year for the next three years and use the proceeds to buy other stocks. But make sure you stick with your plan. The consequence of not following through may result in a portfolio that is tens if not hundreds of thousands of dollars smaller in the long run.

Keep Your Portfolio at Arm's Length

Taking a dispassionate view of your portfolio can also help. I know it is your hard-earned money in there, but a hard-nosed, dispassionate style of investing is best. Don't take it personally when a stock you own declines. These things happen, sometimes for hard-to-understand reasons. On the other hand, don't grow attached to the stock that has doubled since you bought it. It could turn down on you tomorrow. A stock is only as good as your analysis tells you it is. Never fall into the trap of managing your portfolio as if you are cultivating a circle of friends.

COMPANY AND INDUSTRY DIVERSIFICATION

VALUE INVESTING TIPS

▼ Always remain humble about your stock picking ability, and don't concentrate your portfolio in a few stocks.

▼ Invest an equal amount in 10 to 20 stocks that are drawn from at least half a dozen unrelated industries.

▼ Maintain this equal weighting through time by periodically trimming excessively large positions.

The financial benefit of a properly diversified portfolio is one of the most widely held beliefs among practitioners and researchers alike. A properly diversified portfolio produces better risk/return results than does an undiversified portfolio. Thus an investor is better off with a diversified portfolio. This may seem counterintuitive to the uninitiated. After all, you are on your way to being a value investor, so why not focus strictly on selecting the very best stocks and forget about diversifying? Let's look at two good reasons why you should consider diversifying as a value investor.

Being Humble about Stock Picking

First, you need to be humble about your ability to select stocks even as a value investor. Under the best of circumstances, stock picking is a highly unpredictable proposition, fraught with short-term uncertainties and extended dry spells. A properly diversified portfolio represents the foundation upon which you will overlay your own style of value investing. Under no circumstances should you be so confident in your stock picking skills that you invest all your money in a single stock or even a few stocks, because there is no evidence to support such a radical strategy. Instead, value investing represents the frosting on the "cake" of a properly diversified portfolio; it tells you which stocks to buy, not how many to buy nor how much to invest in each.

Benefiting from the Economy

Second, the major source of return in the stock market is the performance of the economy itself. By properly diversifying, you make sure that you will participate in the long-term success of the economy and, in turn, the market. In constructing your portfolio, you are seeking the ideal mix between economy-driven performance and stock picking performance.

At one extreme you could decide to purchase all stocks in the market and weight them according to their market value. Known as an *index portfolio,* its performance is determined exclusively by the overall performance of the stock market and not by individual stock performance. At the other extreme you could invest everything in one stock and thus bet on the singular performance of this one company. In practice, you are seeking the right balance between these two extremes. Your long-term performance will improve when you use value investing in the context of a properly diversified portfolio.

How Many Stocks Are Enough?

Consider including 10 to 20 stocks in your portfolio. It has been well established that the additional benefit of random diversification is nearly zero after a portfolio reaches 20 stocks. In Figure 1.1 note that the risk of the portfolio is little changed after the 20th stock. Also note that there is only a

**FIGURE 1.1 Example of How Diversification
            Can Lower Your Portfolio's Risk**

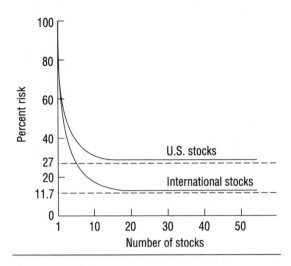

Source: Reprinted with permission from *Financial
Analysts Journal,* July/August 1994. Copyright 1994,
Association for Investment Management and
Research, Charlottesville, VA. All rights reserved.

small change after the 10th stock, thus the sug-
gested portfolio of 10 to 20 stocks.

Industry Diversification

A further step is to draw the 10 to 20 stocks from
at least half a dozen industries. Even better, choose
unrelated industries. For example, if you already
have an auto stock in your portfolio, then invest
next in a biotech company rather than in a steel
company (assuming equal value). A diverse universe of industries ensures adequate portfolio
diversification.

Equal Weighting

A simple way to manage diversification over time
is to keep roughly an equal dollar amount invested

in each stock. If you have ten stocks, then have roughly 10 percent of the portfolio in each stock at all times. If a position should reach 20 percent of the portfolio, then consider paring it back to 10 percent.

Besides keeping the portfolio properly diversified over time, this approach is a subtle way to take advantage of the so-called "small firm effect," the well-established tendency of smaller stocks to out-perform larger stocks, a topic covered in more detail in Chapter 3. By equally weighting, you are increasing the relative importance of the smaller stocks in your portfolio as compared to market weighting the stocks.

Use Mutual Funds To Help You Diversify

What if you don't have enough money to invest in 10 to 20 stocks? The average NYSE stock price is around $25, and if you purchase in round lots (which minimizes transactions costs), then a 10-stock portfolio requires about $25,000 while a 20-stock portfolio requires about $50,000. To some extent you can avoid this problem by investing in low-priced stocks, but this may not be the type of stock in which you wish to invest.

Another solution is to invest a portion of your money in an indexed stock mutual fund and a portion in individual stocks. The index fund provides the diversification while your portfolio is growing to an adequate size. The other advantage of starting out with some money in an indexed mutual fund and some in individual stocks is to see if you like the task of managing your own portfolio. After doing your own portfolio management for a while, you may prefer to turn this sometimes tedious job over to someone else.

Diversification in Large Portfolios

If your portfolio measures in the millions or even the tens of millions of dollars, should you invest in more than 10 to 20 stocks? The answer is no. For individuals, the size of the portfolio does not affect whether they invest in a larger number of stocks. However, when I say this to people, they point to mutual funds that often invest in hundreds of different stocks. One reason mutual funds do this is that they are large enough to affect adversely the market price of the stock they are trading. Thus they find it necessary to spread their sometimes billions of dollars among a large number of stocks to minimize unfavorable market price impacts. I know of very few individual investors who face this particular problem!

INTERNATIONAL DIVERSIFICATION

VALUE INVESTING TIPS

▼ Shoot for a reasonable target of 25 percent to 50 percent of your stock portfolio in international stocks.

▼ Unlike in the domestic portion of your portfolio, where value investing plays a central role, follow more of a buy-and-hold strategy in the international portion by purchasing mutual funds or ADRs.

▼ Don't let currency fluctuations stand in your way; these wash out over time.

As we saw in the last section, some simple planning can help you enjoy the major benefits of company and industry diversification. After properly diversifying your domestic portfolio, is it really necessary also to diversify internationally? The answer to this question is a forceful yes!

Reducing Risk Through International Diversification

A properly diversified international portfolio is less risky than a single market portfolio, such as one invested entirely in NYSE stocks. Figure 1.1 clearly demonstrates the risk reduction benefit of diversifying internationally.

Diversifying internationally seems to confuse investors. Because international investing carries a greater exposure to currency risk, how can you include a riskier stock in your portfolio and actually *reduce* the overall risk of the portfolio? The key to this puzzle is that even though foreign markets carry more risk than U.S. markets do, the risk is largely unrelated to U.S. stock market risk. Thus when you include international stocks in your American portfolio, the risk vanishes inside the combined portfolio and the risk results reported in Figure 1.1 are obtained.

For example, imagine that you are investing in a coin flip that pays $25 if it lands heads and $0 if it lands tails. Assume the price of this "investment" is $10. If you invest in a single coin flip, you are exposed to a great deal of risk, facing a profit of $15 or a loss of $10. However, if you instead invest in a large number of coin flips, then your profit approaches a certain $2.50 per $10 invested. Purchasing enough risky, yet unrelated coin flips reduces your portfolio risk to near zero.

Now you will not be so fortunate to find completely unrelated investments like the coin flips described above. But the benefit of investing internationally is that U.S. stocks, on average, are less related to international stocks than to other U.S. stocks. That is why the international line in Figure 1.1 dips lower than does the U.S. line.

Increasing Return Through International Diversification

Interestingly, when you add international stocks to your portfolio, expected returns are increasing while risk is being reduced. If you accept for the moment that your long-term return in the market is determined by the underlying economic performance (see Chapter 5 for details), then foreign stock markets have an excellent chance of outperforming their U.S. counterparts. This is because the U.S. economy is the largest and most successful in the world. It is therefore hard for the U.S. economy to exceed its long-term growth rate of 3 percent in inflation-adjusted terms. However, other countries can exceed this growth rate because they are in the process of catching up with the United States.

In a manner of speaking, we can think of the United States as the icebreaker of the world economy, opening up a new path for other nations to follow. If these nations get their economic acts together, they will be able to grow their economies at a faster rate than the U.S. economy. The best examples are the "Tigers" of Asia—Korea, Taiwan, Singapore, Hong Kong and, more recently, China. Of course, nothing is for certain, but many nations now seem to have strong economic prospects and as a result very attractive stock return potential.

The Risk and Return Benefits of International Investing

So diversifying internationally makes sense, as shown in Figure 1.2. For the same level of risk, an internationally diversified portfolio can on average earn about 200 basis points more in return. Over an extended investment period this can amount to a substantial amount of additional money.

To obtain the results in Figure 1.2, an investor has to diversify completely. This means that a U.S. investor would have to invest about 70 percent of the portfolio outside the U.S.! In my seminars when

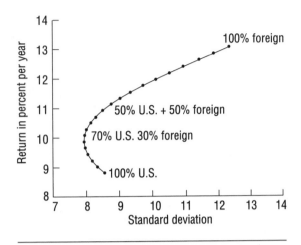

Source: B. Solnik, *International Investments,* © 1996 Addison-Wesley Publishing Company Inc. Reprinted by permission of Addison-Wesley Longman Publishing Company, Inc.

I ask my audience how many have diversified to this extent, very few hands go up. Even professional managers who are quite familiar with these benefits do not come anywhere close to this level of diversification. So don't feel too badly if you have not yet made the move. But do commit yourself to diversifying your portfolio internationally in the future. From 25 percent to 50 percent of your stock portfolio invested internationally is a reasonable target.

Can You Use Value Investing for International Stocks?

How do you go about diversifying internationally? Unfortunately you cannot apply value investing in making international investment decisions. Value investing requires that you have access to reliable and consistent information about stocks. However, in the international arena, such information is not available. Accounting and reporting standards vary from country to country. In general, the United States has some of the most extensive and rigorous reporting standards in the world, but even ours are sometimes lacking. So applying value investing to other country's stocks is currently not feasible. When the equivalent of *Value Line* or *Standard & Poor's* is available in each country around the world, international value investing will become a reality.

International Mutual Funds

You can choose from dozens of international mutual funds. My own preference is to select a low-load fund and be represented in Asia, Europe and emerging markets. Avoid the so-called world funds, which include investments in the United States as part of their portfolio. You are investing in an international mutual fund as a way to diversify your domestic portfolio. With world funds investing in the United States, you defeat this purpose because you are duplicating the already existing U.S. portion of your portfolio.

American Depositary Receipts

An American depositary receipt (ADR) is a hybrid security in which foreign shares are deposited with a bank and an ADR is issued against this deposit. The ADR dollar price fluctuates directly with the underlying foreign stock price and the currency exchange rate. Currently over 2,000 ADRs are available on the NYSE and elsewhere, and each must follow set reporting standards. But be aware that the country-to-country variation in accounting rules mentioned above is just as much a problem with ADRs as it is with the direct purchase of foreign stocks. As a result, it is not possible to apply value investing to ADRs.

Is Purchasing U.S. Multinationals Adequate?

I am regularly asked if buying U.S. stocks that are internationally diversified in their business activities (e.g., IBM generates over 50 percent of their profits outside the United States) results in a sufficiently diversified portfolio. While buying such companies is a move in the right direction, studies show that there is nothing like the real thing: buying foreign stocks themselves. There are two reasons for this.

1. *First, part of the risk of owning stocks is that psychological factors in each country's market drive prices up and down.* Diversifying internationally allows you to reduce this risk because each market is subject to its own generally independent set of psychological forces. The one best remembered exception to this was Black Monday, October 19, 1987, when all world markets fell together. In reality, foreign stock markets are quite unrelated to one another. Buying U.S. companies does not allow you to eliminate this risk because they are traded on U.S. stock exchanges and are thus subject to the same set of psychological forces.

2. *The second reason is that your international diversification is determined by the mixture of the domestic stocks purchased.* Each country's economic and business structure is different, so focusing on U.S. companies will cause you to miss the unique and probably profitable business structure that exists elsewhere. For example, the United States is a service/information economy, and the best investments tend to lie in this sector. Other economies are manufacturing based, so the best investment opportunities lie in this sector while still other countries are agriculturally based. One economic pattern does not fit all countries.

Currency Risk

The final issue that seems to disturb many investors is currency risk. You can deal with this risk in two ways.

1. *First, you can simply ignore it!* Now this seems a very cavalier attitude because currency movements of 10 percent or 20 percent or even 50 percent are not uncommon. In fact, when compared to currency markets, the stock market looks downright rational! But much of what happens in the currency markets is noise (see the next section for more details) and thus fades away over time. Since 1973, when the current regime of floating exchange rates came into existence, the dollar has changed very little in value on a trade-weighted basis even though its value has fluctuated wildly from year to year during this 20-year period.
2. *The second way to deal with currency risk is to purchase a mutual fund that hedges currency risk.* This will provide you with short-term peace of mind and will probably have little or no impact on the long-term performance of your portfolio.

MANAGING YOUR PORTFOLIO OVER TIME

VALUE INVESTING TIPS

▼ If you manage your portfolio too actively, you will be responding to noise; if you manage it too inactively, you will be missing the buy and sell signals.

▼ Aim for an average holding period of from three to five years, which translates into an average annual turnover rate of around 25 percent per year.

▼ One of your challenges is to find the frequency of analysis that will allow you to reach these targets.

How often should you spruce up your portfolio? Every day, every month, every year or every ten years whether you need to or not? While every ten years may seem absurd, it is closer to the truth than you might think! Most investors are *too* active. Your challenge is to develop a trading style that allows you to separate the wheat from the chaff or separate the "signal" from the "noise."

A Sea of Noise

Anyone who follows the market on a daily basis immediately notices a great deal of volatility. The market gyrates over a range of 100 points or more during a typical day. After the fact, you will hear or read some expert opinion on why the market did what it did. Although this "Monday morning quarterbacking" often sounds plausible, a careful analysis shows that almost all of what transpires in the market on a daily basis is noise. *Noise* is defined as stock price movements that cannot be explained by changes in underlying economic or financial fundamentals. To the greatest extent possible you want to avoid making decisions based on noise.

Noisy Black Monday

For example, let's focus for a moment on Black Monday, October 19, 1987. In a library on that day one of my students ran up to tell me that the stock market had just dropped 500 points. I looked him squarely in the eye and said, "Haven't I taught you better? The stock market can't possibly drop 500 points!" In spite of this admonishment, he persisted. So I checked with a librarian. Naturally I was dumbstruck! Not only had I lost tens of thousands of dollars in my portfolio, but I had also lost my career! Nobody would want to listen to me talk about the stock market after it had dropped 500 points! What would I ever do? But after I had a good meal and a good night's sleep, the anxiety passed.

In retrospect, how should we view the Black Monday stock market crash? It probably wouldn't surprise you to find out that this single event is the most thoroughly studied in all of stock market history. A virtual who's who of the finance world has studied and written about Black Monday. And what did all this modern day brain power conclude? We have no idea what caused Black Monday! In other words, it is the most spectacular noise event ever recorded! If something as dramatic as Black Monday is a noise event, then it is not too hard to accept that many if not most stock price movements are in reality noise events.

The Value Investor's Target Holding Period

The truth is that a buy or sell signal can easily get lost in the noise of the stock market, but detecting such signals is the key to value investing. The *signal* is the relationship between value and price (i.e., buy undervalued stocks, sell overvalued stocks). Trying to detect a faint signal in the noisy background of the stock market means that you will have to adopt a very patient style. How patient? I suggest that you aim for an average holding period of from three to five years. This means that portfolio turnover should average around 25 percent per year.

The Impact of the Business Cycle

The business cycle is the basis for this three-year to five-year holding period. At a business cycle peak, the market tends to be overvalued, while at a trough, it tends to be undervalued. Since World

War II, the average length of the business cycle has been about five years. Thus by pursuing value investing, you are trying to capture the effect of the business cycle on the valuation of individual stocks, and consequently you will be holding stocks for an average of from three to five years.

Does this mean that you should hold a stock for a minimum of three years and a maximum of five years? In general, no. The actual holding period will depend on the stock's undervalued to overvalued cycle. Although averaging five years, the length of the business cycle is in reality quite variable from cycle to cycle (since WWII, the shortest cycle was 28 months while the longest was 100 months). But more importantly, the stock's valuation cycle depends on a number of other factors, such as industry trends and management decisions, that may be little influenced by the business cycle. The result is that an actual holding period may range from as short as six months to as long as ten years or more. Over an extended period, it should average from three to five years.

How Often Should You Look at Your Portfolio?

Finally, how often should you look at and analyze your portfolio? It takes considerable effort to analyze your portfolio and potential new stocks. The real temptation is that when you put in this amount of work, you feel like you should do "something" with your portfolio. I have often said that one of the problems faced by professional portfolio managers is that they work full time. Because it is very easy for them to look at their portfolio many times a day, this frequency increases the chance of their responding to noise. The high average turnover and on average poor performance of these managers support this contention.

You will have to decide, then, how often you can look at your portfolio and still avoid overtrading. I have talked to investors who look at their portfolio every day but still trade infrequently. Others find it necessary, for any number of reasons, to restrict their frequency of analysis. Find the best mix for you.

MEASURING PORTFOLIO PERFORMANCE

VALUE INVESTING TIPS

▼ The proof of the pudding is the long-term performance of your portfolio relative to a properly selected benchmark portfolio.

▼ Do not focus on the performance of individual stocks.

▼ While value investing allows you to increase the chances of selecting winning stocks, you will still pick your fair share of losers.

Some time ago I prepared a performance summary for a client showing that her portfolio had outperformed the market over the previous year. The meeting went smoothly until we encountered a stock that had dropped to a price near zero (the "walking dead" as these stocks are often dubbed). "Tom, how about this stock?" she asked as she pointed to the worthless stock. I explained that even though she had lost nearly everything in this particular stock, her overall portfolio had done well. "How about this stock?" she asked a second time even more emphatically. I knew I was in trouble. Even though I explained again that portfolio performance, not the performance of each individual stock, was important, the next day I was fired!

Portfolio Versus Individual Stock Performance

Like my former client, investors quite often focus on individual stock performance. After all, you are purchasing individual stocks, so why not measure the performance in that same way? The reality is, however, you are implementing a value style of investing. This is the *theme* of your portfolio. Individual stocks are simply the means by which you are implementing this theme. You are not trying to pick winning stocks per se. Instead you are trying to implement a winning style, that is, you are value investing.

There is actually a real danger in focusing on individual stock performance. Investors have told me that they will never buy a particular stock because the stock performed poorly the last time they bought it. Such an investment approach focuses on avoiding disasters. The problem is that by trying to avoid disasters, investors are forsaking upside potential. Value investing allows you to increase your chances of selecting winning stocks, but along the way you are going to select your fair share of losers. It comes with the territory.

Measuring Performance

So how do you measure your portfolio's performance? Most important, you need to measure the *total* return on your portfolio, including dividends paid, realized gains and losses, *and* unrealized gains and losses. Some will argue incorrectly that you should not include unrealized gains. But you should include all sources of return when calculating the total return for your portfolio.

One of the complications of calculating a return occurs when money is moving in and out of the portfolio. The best way to handle this problem is to calculate the return between the points when money is moved in or out of the portfolio. Accumulating the resulting returns over a year's time to estimate the annual return for the portfolio is referred to as a *time-weighted average portfolio return* and gives a clearer measure of performance.

Choosing a Benchmark

For many investors, the S&P 500 Index is the appropriate benchmark. The performance of this index is reported regularly in publications such as *The Wall Street Journal, Investor's Business Daily* and *Barron's*. Make sure that you include the dividend yield, which is usually between 2 percent and 3 percent. For example, the most commonly reported number is the price change for the S&P 500, so the S&P 500 dividend yield would have to be added to obtain the correct performance benchmark.

If you have a lower risk portfolio, you could use a lower risk benchmark such as the S&P Utilities. If you have a higher risk portfolio, then use a higher risk benchmark such as the Nasdaq Composite. A wide range of index portfolios are available, so you should be able to find one that closely matches the risk characteristics of your particular portfolio.

How Well Have You Done?

Once you have selected the benchmark, you can measure the relative performance of your portfolio. Simply put, you want to outperform your benchmark. Even under the best of circumstances, you will not be able to beat the market every year. However, over time you want your average return to be higher than that of the benchmark.

You should measure relative performance over a period of time that is longer than five years or one business cycle. From a purely hard-nosed perspective, if you have not beaten the market, you should not be spending your time managing your own portfolio. However, even if performance is not superior, the intrinsic rewards of making your own decisions may be enough. This is a choice you will have to make.

CHAPTER 2

▼ ▼ ▼

Tilting the Market in Your Favor

VALUE INVESTOR'S CHECKLIST

✓ If you are patient and carefully sift through the noise of the market, you will see discernible market patterns.

✓ Because most market patterns occur over several years, you will not capture the potential benefit by frequent trading.

✓ The *small-firm effect* is the result of smaller stocks outperforming larger stocks, after adjusting for risk differences.

✓ The *low price-to-earnings ratio effect*, in which low PE stocks outperform high PE stocks, is at the very heart of value investing.

✓ The *neglected-firm effect* involves the mispricing of stocks resulting from the lack of analyst coverage.

✓ There is significant overlap among these three effects as low PE firms tend to be small firms that also tend to have less analyst coverage.

UNDERSTANDING PATTERNS IN MARKET RETURNS

VALUE INVESTING TIPS

▼ The market tends to be overvalued during times of economic expansion and undervalued during recessions.

▼ Unlike returns, changes in market volatility seem to be largely random.

▼ The stock market, contrary to economic theory, performs poorly during periods of rapidly rising inflation.

The history of stock market returns is one of the great success stories of all time. An investment of $1 in the stock market in 1802 would have grown to $3 million by 1992! In contrast, the same investment in bonds would have resulted in a portfolio worth a mere $6,600. As we will discuss in Chapter 5, the phenomenal success of the stock market simply reflects the amazing success of the U.S. economy over this same time period. Figure 2.1 shows the return history for the stock, bond, Treasury bill and the gold markets relative to the inflation rate. Clearly the stock market is the all-time investment champion!

How Market Returns Vary over Time

How do stock market returns change over time, and how does this affect the way you invest in

FIGURE 2.1   Total Nominal Return Indexes (1802–1992)

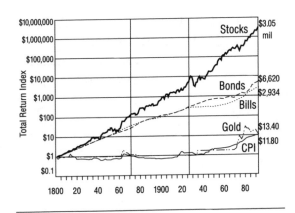

Source: *Stocks for the Long Run* by Jeremy J. Siegel. Copyright Richard D. Irwin Co., 1994. Used with permission.

stocks? Let's begin by taking a closer look at returns over shorter periods of time.

The data in Figure 2.2 shows that real (i.e., net of inflation) stock market returns have been amazingly stable over the three subperiods: 1802–1870, 1871–1925, and 1926–1992. These subperiods roughly correspond to the three major economic periods in U.S. history: the agrarian period, the industrial period and the services/information, world power period.

What is so interesting about these results is that, regardless of the type of economy generating the returns, the average real return has remained at right around 7 percent. This is powerful support for the tremendous stability and vitality of the U.S. financial and economic system regardless of what is being produced by the economy. These are very encouraging results because a properly diversified portfolio is the starting point for value investing.

FIGURE 2.2 Historical Real Stock Market Returns

Major Subperiods:	1802–1870	1871–1925	1926–1992
Real Return	7.0%	6.6%	6.6%
Inflation Rate	0.1	0.6	3.1

Source: *Stocks for the Long Run* by Jeremy J. Siegel. Copyright Richard D. Irwin Co., 1994. Used with permission.

The Impact of Inflation on Value Investing

Another very positive message in Figure 2.2 is that over long periods of time, the stock market is an excellent inflation hedge. The inflation rate rose from 0.1 percent to 0.6 percent to 3.1 percent over these three subperiods, yet the real return was virtually the same in all three subperiods.

But few of us have a 70-year investment horizon, so let's get more realistic! Figure 2.3 reports results for two subperiods since World War II: 1966–1981 and 1982–1992. Instead of a changing economy, these two periods represent clearly different inflationary periods: the first characterized by rising inflation and the second by falling inflation. The impact on real returns is dramatic. In the first period, the real return is a paltry –0.4 percent while during the second period, it is a strong 11.1 percent. Thus over shorter periods, changing inflationary expectations can have a dramatic impact on returns.

Should you alter your strategy based on inflationary expectations? As we will discuss in Chapter 5, the Federal Reserve's monetary policy (basically the decision of how much money should be created) is of great interest to you. The greatest danger is that the Fed, in trying to fine tune the economy, inadvertently ignites a new round of high inflation. Such a mistake could devastate your stock portfolio. But beyond this mega-mistake by the Fed, small

FIGURE 2.3   The Impact of Inflation on Real Stock Market Returns

Major Subperiods:	1966–1981	1982–1992
Real Return	–0.4%	11.1%
Inflation Rate	7.0	3.8

Source: *Stocks for the Long Run* by Jeremy J. Siegel. Copyright Richard D. Irwin Co., 1994. Used with permission.

variations in inflation that have occurred in recent years are probably unimportant for making investment decisions. But you must remain vigilant with respect to the actions of the Federal Reserve.

The Impact of Economic Cycles

Beyond the impact of inflation, several economic and market-wide measures seem to predict average returns. These include market dividend yield, the premium of the Treasury bond interest rate over the T-bill rate, the premium of the corporate bond rate over the T-bond rate and the growth in industrial production. Chapter 5 will discuss the specifics of these relationships. For now, the relationship to keep in mind is that the stock market tends to be overvalued when the economy is growing strongly and undervalued when the economy is in a recession.

What about Risk?

In addition to considering return, risk also plays a prominent role in the market. Does the level of market risk change over time? The clear answer is yes. But unlike return, the changes in risk do not seem to show any particular pattern. Experts have noted that the stock market was considerably more volatile during the Great Depression than at any other time in its history. Beyond this observation, almost nothing can be said about how market risk changes over time.

More recently, the stock market crash of 1987 comes to mind as a time of elevated volatility (by some measures, five times the level of normal volatility!). But again there is no generally agreed upon explanation for this increase in volatility. Risk measures returned to normal levels within six months of the 1987 crash.

As unnerving as such episodes are, there seems to be no way to predict them, nor is there a rational portfolio response to them. You should consider them a short-term unpleasantness you have to endure to reap the market's long-term benefits.

ARE STOCKS EVER MISPRICED?

VALUE INVESTING TIPS

▼ Despite its intuitive appeal, there is virtually no support that technical analysis of stocks works.

▼ Studies find that economy-wide information and most firm-specific information are not useful in making investment decisions.

▼ Even professional money managers are not immune to the underperformance plague, as they are often forced to respond to the marginal "hot money" investor who is ready to bolt from the fund at the first hint of underperformance.

▼ You don't face such pressures, so you can stick with value investing through thick and thin; consequently you have a better chance of outperforming the market than do the professionals.

The primary conclusion of a large number of *market efficiency* studies, mostly conducted by academics, is that it is virtually impossible for you to earn an exceptional return. The resulting recommendation is that you should simply purchase an index portfolio and forget about active management. This advice is tantamount to saying that diversification is the *only* thing that matters when constructing a portfolio.

While your instincts might say that you should reject this seemingly absurd conclusion, the evidence in support of so-called market efficiency is both thorough and compelling. *Market efficiency* simply means that stocks are always correctly priced. The evidence can be broken down into three broad categories: (1) evidence regarding simple trading rules, (2) evidence regarding economic and firm specific information and (3) evidence regarding the performance of investment professionals.

The Evidence Against Simple Trading Rules

The most common trading rule is the *filter rule*. For example, one popular filter rule says to sell when the stock rises by 20 percent or falls by 10 percent. Such rules seem to resonate with many investors and can be easily justified on intuitive grounds. The spoken variation of this rule is to let your winners run while cutting your losses. As appealing as these rules seem, no support exists that they actually improve your returns. In fact, just the opposite seems to be the case. The upper and lower bounds trigger selling which incurs transaction costs. Consequently, net returns decline by the amount of these transaction costs. The major benefit of the filter rule seems to accrue to your broker!

Numerous other studies of simple trading rules involving moving averages, support levels, resistance levels, triple bottoms and the like have come to the same conclusion. You probably have recognized these as some of the primary tools of technical analysis. *Technical analysis* attempts to divine short-term price movements so that you can earn above-average returns. Unfortunately, no evidence exists supporting the usefulness of technical analysis.

Now you may object to this conclusion. By following a stock over time, you know that the price wanders for no apparent fundamental reason. It is therefore tempting to turn to something like technical analysis, for it is the only method that attempts to explain these short-term price wanderings. And if you feel it is important to remain "on top" of your portfolio at all times, then technical analysis is a match made in heaven. But while indulging your need for continuous control, you are probably making decisions based on noise. Again the evidence supports the contention that you are more than likely enriching your broker and not your own portfolio!

Evidence on Economic and Firm-Specific Information

You are constantly being bombarded with news about the economy and individual firms. You might feel compelled to keep up with this torrent of information and probably have a vague sense of anxiety when you don't. You will be happy to learn that even if you could keep up with all this news, it probably wouldn't help because prices already reflect this information by the time you receive it.

Economy-wide information. The evidence on employment, inflation and money supply reveals that the stock market reacts about six months in advance. So unless you are able to forecast the economy further than six months into the future, keeping track of economic information is not a productive use of your time.

Firm-specific information. Literally hundreds of studies, called *event studies,* have shown that firm-specific information is impounded very rapidly into prices. In fact, share prices reflect certain

dramatic events such as a merger announcement up to two weeks prior to the announcement date. So who says insiders don't have an advantage over the rest of us?

The bottom line, then, is that economic and most firm-specific information are not going to be of much help to you. Note that I said most, not all, firm-specific information. Shortly we will look at the kinds of information that might indeed be helpful.

The Evidence on the Performance of Investment Professionals

If in fact stocks are at times mispriced, then investment professionals such as mutual fund managers, pension fund managers and Wall Street analysts should be able to exploit these mistakes and earn above-average returns. After all, they spend the whole day gathering information, analyzing this information and keeping track of the market.

But alas, the studies are no kinder to the professionals than they are to the simple trading rules. Where there is a considerable amount of information about performance, such as for mutual funds and pension funds, we find that on average professionals underperform the market.

Of course many investment professionals do not have a public performance record. Is it possible that the really good managers are somewhere out there in this dark forest? Maybe. But the bad news is that every time we get a glimpse into this uncharted area, we find out that the newly discovered portfolio managers actually have feet of clay.

Why Many Professional Managers Underperform

To understand why professional portfolio managers do so poorly on average, you need to understand how they are compensated. The vast majority of portfolio managers are paid as a percentage of assets under management. The larger the asset base, the greater the compensation. Thus managers are quite sensitive to a decrease in the dollars under management. So a quarter or two of bad performance can be very damaging because some of the money, maybe a lot of the money, will desert the fund after such a down period. Thus the *marginal* investor, sometimes referred to as a "hot money" investor, has a significant impact on the investment strategy of the manager.

Many managers therefore start changing strategies to match the current theme of the market. Such themes include value, growth, cyclicals, interest sensitive and asset plays, to name a few. But of all these themes, the only one that has shown any kind of staying power is *value investing*. While the other themes might work over shorter periods, their long-term performance is poor. Thus theme switching requires the ability to time the theme fairly accurately. The evidence seems to say that this is indeed difficult.

So why don't managers simply stay with value investing? The reason is that, even though it works over the longer term, it can perform poorly over shorter periods. In fact, my own and others' work reveals that value investing can underperform the market for periods as long as five years. Even much shorter dry spells will probably cause a manager to abandon a technique.

Hope for the Individual Investor

Of course, as an individual investor you don't face the problem of marginal investors ready to bolt at the first hint of underperformance (some attendees at my seminars tell me that their spouse plays this particular role!). Your only goal is to earn the highest return over your investment horizon. Thus you can stick with value investing through thick and thin.

In fact this is one of the major themes of this book: As an individual investor, you have a better chance of outperforming the market than does the professional. If you resist the temptation of changing strategies when things are not going well, then you have an excellent chance of beating the pros over the longer term.

I believe this is even more the case today as institutional investors make up a growing share of the market. That means a smaller percentage of the money will be in the hands of individual investors who are the ones most able to stick with value investing. This bodes well for the continued future viability of value investing.

Well, Is the Market Efficient?

The answer is both yes and no. Most information is indeed rapidly reflected in stock prices, so you should not spend your time following and analyzing this information. But the information inherent in value investing does not seem to be rapidly reflected in stock prices and so is worth spending time on. This information is the focus of the remainder of this book.

CATCHING THE TRADE WINDS OF THE MARKET

VALUE INVESTING TIPS

▼ Although brutally efficient much of the time, the market does have a few tendencies that are worth knowing about.

▼ A number of studies show that you should focus on small stocks, low PE stocks and stocks with low institutional holdings or low analyst coverage.

▼ By setting your portfolio sails to capture these market trade winds, you will improve the chances of successfully selecting value stocks.

The last section painted a pretty bleak picture for those wishing to actively manage their own portfolios. However, things aren't quite as bad as they first seem. Besides the many studies that have shown the market to be correctly priced much of the time, a growing body of research shows that the market also makes mistakes. Let's look at this more promising group of studies.

Identifying Superior Performance

The issue of determining what works involves separating the noise from the signal. This can be accomplished only with very large samples in which the noise averages out. Conclusions based on small samples are very susceptible to noise bias. But by their very nature, every portfolio manager's performance record is a small sample. What is the sample size needed to neutralize noise bias? The answer is from 50 to 100 years of performance data!

Having said this, we are all well aware that many, if not most, investors are willing to accept a much shorter period as proof of superior performance. My own observations indicate that a performance record as short as two years, if dramatic enough, is enough to attract huge sums of money to a professional manager. But the truth is that for such short periods, it is all but impossible to tell whether the superior performance represents skill or luck.

You have a better chance of identifying something that works by using a very large sample over a very long time period. This means that you have to give up the hope of ever identifying a superior manager. Even if they exist, the time periods over which they are active are too short to accurately identify them as superior. Even Peter Lynch's fabled performance while at Fidelity Magellan was indistinguishable from noise even though he outperformed the market by an average of 10.5 percent over a 13-year period!

Thus you have to focus on those market and individual stock characteristics that stand the test of time and noise rather than focus on identifying superior managers. But, of course, that is fine because you are trying to develop your own management style. Let's now turn to this task.

Taking Advantage of Market Anomalies

As you guide your portfolio through the turbulent weather and seas of the market, you would like to set your sails to the most advantageous position. This represents a real challenge as you watch the market swell and recede and millions of investors roil the market on a continuous basis. But you can find opportunities to preplan your course and set your sails accordingly.

Although the market is brutally efficient most of the time, it is, after all, a human institution, susceptible to human emotions. There are good reasons to believe that the market does indeed make mistakes by overreacting to some kinds of information. Value investing attempts to take advantage of these overreactions. Beyond using the value investing techniques described later in this book, are there pervasive market tendencies of which you should be aware? And how do you go about setting the sails of your portfolio to take advantage of these market trade winds?

Small Firm Effect

One of the most interesting market trade winds is the so-called small-firm effect. Numerous studies demonstrate that small-firm stocks produce higher returns than those of larger firms. Typically firm size is measured by market capitalization (shares outstanding × price per share). Blindly investing in the smallest quintile of stocks traded on the NYSE and AMEX seems to produce an average return improvement of 2 percent to 3 percent over a market index portfolio (i.e., a 12 percent to 13 percent average return compared to 10 percent for the index). And this is after adjusting for the additional risk inherent in the small stock portfolio.

FIGURE 2.4 Size Distribution by Market

Number of Companies in Each
Exchange and Percentage

Size Quintiles ($ Millions)	NYSE	AMEX	Nasdaq National	Nasdaq Small Cap	
$0–20	42 (2%)	206 (33%)	805 (22%)	291 (67%)	
$20–62	119 (6%)	192 (31%)	958 (26%)	80 (18%)	
$62–165	283 (14%)	123 (20%)	903 (25%)	36 (8%)	
$165–560	571 (29%)	66 (11%)	689 (19%)	19 (4%)	
$560–107,000	976 (49%)	36 (6%)	327 (9%)	7 (2%)	
					Grand Total
Total	1,991	623	3,682	433	6,729

Source: *AAII Stock Investor,* January 1996. Used with permission.

The evidence on the small-firm effect is robust over the full range of firm size. This means that you do not have to invest in the smallest stocks to exploit this effect. All you have to do is invest in *smaller* stocks. If you focus your efforts on income stocks, for example, then choose the *smaller* income stocks. If you focus on blue chip stocks, then choose the *smaller* blue chip stocks. If you focus on value stocks, then choose the *smaller* value stocks. Whatever your preferred strategy, moving to *smaller* stocks will enhance your returns.

The information in Figure 2.4 provides a picture of the firm size range for four different stock markets: the NYSE, the AMEX, the Nasdaq National Market and the Nasdaq Small Cap market. You will find a considerable range in firm size within each of these four markets. Thus it is possible for you to select stocks based on firm size regardless of which market is your focus.

Finding information about smaller stocks may present a problem. If you limit yourself to NYSE stocks, then a considerable amount of information is available through sources such as *Value Line Investment Survey* and *S&P Stock Reports*. If you focus on AMEX stocks, a considerable amount of information is still available, but some AMEX stocks will be hard to research. If you go to the extreme of limiting your search to Nasdaq small cap stocks, then you may be limited to reading the annual report. Many investors find this unacceptable because the annual report often contains little useful information beyond the financial statements. Thus as you move down the size scale, you are also moving down the information scale. You have to decide where to stop. But do consider moving down in size as far as possible.

The Low PE Effect

On average, stocks with low price-to-earnings, or PE, ratios (price per share ÷ earnings per share) tend to outperform high PE stocks. So whenever possible, you should construct your portfolio to take advantage of this effect. In fact the concept of value investing is closely associated with low PE investing. In Chapter 8, we will look at various value investing techniques that go beyond low PE investing.

You can capture the low PE effect by using other measures as well. Some investors prefer to focus on low price-to-book (PB) ratios, low price-to-sales (PS) ratios and the like. Many ratios involving price and some aspect of fundamental value such as earnings, book value or sales seem to help in identifying value stocks.

What do I mean by a low PE? I consider a low PE to be any stock with a PE of less than ten. This upper boundary on the PE ratio will differ from investor to investor, but you should strive to focus on the lower 20 percent of PE ratios.

The Characteristics of Low PE Stocks

What type of stock do you find in the lower 20 percent of PE ratios? First, you will find a tendency for these stocks to be smaller than average. This means that you may run into the same information shortage problem that you run into when trying to analyze small stocks. But even though on average the stocks are smaller, the low PE group shows a full range of sizes. My own experience is that the lack of information is not a major problem when investing in low PE stocks.

A number of studies have shown that the small size and low PE effects are largely independent of one another. So a portfolio of small, low PE stocks tends to outperform either a small-stock-only portfolio or a low-PE-only portfolio. In fact the best-performing portfolio is comprised of small companies that suffered earnings losses in the previous year (thus sporting a negative PE ratio). This statement always leads to nervous laughter among my seminar participants!

The major concern of investors who spend time analyzing low PE stocks is that the stocks in the lower 20% often don't look very good when carefully analyzed. They tend to be companies having trouble in one form or another: slowing growth, shrinking markets, internal management problems, maybe even a significant chance of default. In many cases, these are not pretty stocks to look at! So if you spend time investing in low PE stocks, you have to have a strong stomach. Not that all low PE stocks are ugly, but a substantial number are. You might ask, "Why not throw out the bad stories and keep the good ones?" Your fear is that this action might eliminate the benefit of investing in low PE stocks. So you are pretty much stuck with stretching your comfort zone if you plan to focus on low PE stocks. But the good news is that studies consistently show that low PE benefits are real.

Neglected-Firm Effect

Stocks are correctly priced much of the time because thousands of investors managing billions of dollars are making their investment decisions after carefully analyzing economic and individual company fundamentals. Thus it might be useful to identify those stocks that a large segment of the market has neglected. Among such stocks, you will be more likely to find mispriced stocks.

How do investors and analysts go about organizing their efforts to analyze stocks? Institutional investors play a significant role in skewing the allocation of analyst efforts. The biggest generators of brokerage fees are institutional investors who trade more actively and in larger blocks than do individuals. Because of their sheer size, institutional investors invest in larger stocks with substantial daily volume. So *large* brokerage firms focus their analysts' time on *large* stocks that are the favorites of *large* institutional investors. Consequently, professional analysts spend an inordinate amount of time on larger stocks due to the demands of their brokerage firm or professional investment manager bosses.

Does this mean that neglected stocks, which tend to be smaller stocks, are more likely to be mispriced? The answer seems to be yes. If you are going to spend time on value investing, why not focus your attention on neglected stocks?

Identifying Neglected Stocks

How do you identify neglected stocks? You can do this in two ways.

1. *First, you can look at the fraction of outstanding shares held by institutional investors*. The idea is that a large percentage of institutional ownership will attract a large amount of analyst coverage for the reasons described above. For the market as a whole, institutional ownership now exceeds individual ownership, so a stock with

50 percent or less institutional ownership is an increasingly neglected stock.

2. *Second, you can look up the number of professional analysts following a particular stock.* This number can range as high as 50 and as low as zero. The smaller the number, the more likely the stock will be neglected. It is more difficult to find the number of analysts than the percentage of institutional holdings, as the latter is more widely reported. For example, *Value Line Investment Survey, S&P Stock Reports* and *AAII Stock Investor* all report institutional ownership of a particular stock, while only the latter one reports the number of analysts covering the stock.

CHAPTER 3

▼ ▼ ▼

Where Do You Get Your Investment Ideas?

VALUE INVESTOR'S CHECKLIST

✓ You can use computer-based as well as noncomputer-based techniques for screening a large stock universe to obtain a manageable number of stocks for further analysis.

✓ Select your stocks from as large and as broad a universe as possible.

✓ If you use your daily lifestyle as a way to select stocks, you will select from a universe that is too narrow.

✓ Use the three effects of small size, low PE and neglected firms described in Chapter 2 for initial value stock screening.

✓ Use growth, profitability and risk as secondary screens.

THE UNIVERSE OF
INVESTMENT IDEAS

VALUE INVESTING TIPS

▼ Don't allow your daily life experiences to limit your investment ideas.

▼ Use a large universe of stocks, such as all those traded on the NYSE or the Nasdaq, to gain exposure to a rich set of investment ideas.

Most investors, both individuals and professionals alike, approach the issue of what universe of stocks to consider with a lot of baggage. Statements like "I don't want to invest in technology stocks because they are too unpredictable" or "I will never invest in oil stocks again because I lost money on them during the 1980s" are standard fare among investors. Remember that your goal is to identify and invest in value stocks. You should let the value investing techniques pick the stocks, and don't eliminate large segments of the market prior to starting this analysis.

Start with a Broad Universe of Stocks

Second only to proper diversification, the universe from which you get your investment ideas is a critical decision. If you prematurely narrow your investment choices, your portfolio is less likely to perform well. Thus it is important to identify the universe and then the method you will use to narrow this universe to a manageable number.

In general, start with the broadest possible universe. For example, you might consider all the stocks traded on the NYSE. Or you might consider the stocks traded on the Nasdaq National Market system (NMS). Or even better, you might consider all stocks on both of these markets.

Your Broker, Your Barber or Your Brother

Where do you get that next investment idea? It is not uncommon to get these ideas from the people around you. I somewhat jokingly refer to this group as your broker, your barber or your brother, or your broker, your hairdresser or your sister. You may have one of these people as a source of investment ideas. Let me tell you about my family.

I have a brother named Ron (not the famous actor-turned-director). Over the years, he has gotten pretty good at picking stocks. One day my mother asked me for some advice on which stock to purchase. I began to regale her on the intricacies of value investing. I noticed that her eyes began to glaze. "Mom, what is wrong?" I asked. Then she said, "I think I will wait to talk to your brother Ron." I was cut to the quick!

Do you have your own "brother Ron"? No matter how good he or she is, I recommend that you expand your investment idea universe beyond those you know.

Lifestyle Investing

Another commonly heard recommendation is to stick with what you know. Invest in your own company, buy the stocks of the best products you see in the stores or focus on the companies that provide the best service are common recommendations. Again, I believe that this results in too small a universe. Even for those who travel extensively, a person's daily routine exposes them to a very small slice of the economy. Tens of thousands of companies are traded on various stock markets, and at best you come across only several hundred of these during your daily routine. This is too drastic a reduction.

While it is true that you have to reduce the number of stocks to a manageable number for further consideration, the way in which your daily life is ordered seems a limiting stock filter indeed. Using such a filter probably has more to do with achieving a certain level of comfort than with making hard-nosed investment decisions.

Thus the bottom line is to consider as broad a universe of stocks as possible. By means of the screening techniques that we will look at next, you can obtain a manageable number of stocks that have a better chance of producing above-average returns than if you limit your choices prematurely.

HOW TO SELECT VALUE STOCKS

VALUE INVESTING TIPS

▼ Use a screen to reduce the number of available stocks to those that have the greatest potential for value investing.

▼ Screens based on size, PE and neglect are the most useful.

▼ You may also want to use growth, profitability and risk as secondary screens.

It is only natural to apply your previously learned personal screens to the stock selection process. What are some of these learned screens? They are things such as staying with what is familiar, acting only when there is a considerable amount of favorable information, asking a respected family member or friend for advice or following the professionals. Unfortunately, these do not work well in the investment world. So in developing your own individual stock selection rule, you will have to move beyond what comes naturally.

The Three Effects Revisited

In Chapter 2, I described three market anomalies that will help you select stocks: the small-firm effect, the low PE effect and the neglected-firm effect. Small firms are small based on market value, and they generate larger returns than do large firms. Low PE stocks outperform high PE stocks. And neglected firms are those with little analyst coverage offering better opportunities for being undervalued stocks.

One or all of these three effects are worth considering as screening criteria. There is some overlap among them because low PE stocks also tend to be small stocks and small stocks also tend to be neglected stocks. To show you what to expect when screening based on these three criteria, Figure 3.1 gives a sampling of stocks that have a PE less than 10 and also fall into the smallest 20 percent in terms of size and neglect for both the NYSE and the Nasdaq-NMS. Neglect is measured as the percent of institutional ownership. Based on the empirical evidence, then, the stocks listed in Figure 3.1 represented an interesting starting point for value investing early in 1996.

The Interaction of the Three Effects

The return advantages of these three effects seem to be additive in that small stocks with low PEs have a better return potential than do stocks that are simply small or simply have a low PE. The reality is that *something* in the market seems to be creating above average returns for these particular stocks. This *something* consists of three factors: (1) the size of the company, (2) the PE of the company and (3) the degree of neglect. By using these three together in some combination, you will have this *something* working in your favor. What is this *something*? I believe it is the tendency of markets to price stocks for emotional rather than for fundamental reasons.

FIGURE 3.1   Small, Low PE and Neglected Stocks

Company	Market Cap. ($ Millions)	PE	% Instit. Holdings
NYSE			
Aeroflex, Inc.	45	6.7	22
Asset Investors Corp.	76	5.1	9
Boston Celtics L.P.	127	2.6	0
Chesapeake Utilities	59	9.0	13
CRI Liquidating REIT	110	8.8	1
DDL Electronics, Inc.	39	9.5	6
Great Northern Iron Ore	69	9.0	12
Oriental Bank & Trust	113	9.3	18
Raytech Corporation	12	0.9	21
Rowe Furniture Corp.	59	7.1	12
Scott's Liquid Gold	25	9.5	8
The Sherwood Group, Inc.	111	7.3	9
Torch Energy Royalty Trust	106	5.0	2
Westbridge Capital Corp.	41	7.8	23
Nasdaq			
American Casino Ent.	42	8.5	1
Bancorp Connecticut Inc.	43	9.9	5
China Industrial Group	33	2.6	4
Columbia Bancorp	37	8.5	0
D.I.Y. Home Warehouse	33	9.4	8
Dolco Packaging Corp.	28	6.4	13

FIGURE 3.1 Small, Low PE and Neglected Stocks (Continued)

Company	Market Cap. ($ Millions)	PE	% Instit. Holdings
First Colorado Bancorp	78	6.1	12
Florida First Bancorp	28	9.8	2
Foothill Indep't Bancorp	36	9.5	6
Hampshire Group, Limited	42	5.3	14
Home Federal Bancorp	57	8.6	12
InterContinental Life	59	6.6	4
Investors Title Company	30	9.1	6
Kaye Group Inc.	54	8.3	2
McClain Industries	21	6.4	7
MLX Corporation	29	1.5	7
Noland Company	69	9.4	12
Pac Rim Holding Corp.	24	7.6	10
PVF Capital Corporation	29	8.8	2
SCP Pool Corporation	48	9.6	0
Sirena Apparel Group Inc.	29	5.8	7
TFC Enterprises, Inc.	28	6.7	14
The Somerset Group, Inc.	29	8.1	9
Upper Peninsula Energy	58	9.8	12
Western Beef Inc.	31	6.0	10
Zing Technologies Inc.	28	6.8	9

Source: *AAII Stock Investor,* January 31, 1996. Used with permission.

Why Small Stocks Tend To Be Value Stocks

For example, small stocks are not well known, and not much information is available for these companies. Investors are reluctant to invest in that which is not well known, so the prices of small stocks are artificially depressed.

However, it is important to keep in mind that knowing a lot about a company or the market does not guarantee a superior return. Recall the typical professional portfolio manager described in Chapter 2 who spends a great deal of time following the market and yet underperforms the market. In that manager's case, knowledge does not translate into returns. The converse is also the case: The lack of knowledge does not translate into poor returns. Again consider an index fund manager who spends no time studying the market and yet earns the market return. Consequently, the lack of information may not be a good reason for avoiding a stock.

Why PE Stocks Tend To Be Value Stocks

In the case of low PE stocks, often an unpleasant story is associated with the company, such as low growth potential, poor economic prospects, high debt levels, poor industry performance and others. Such stocks tend to be undervalued because investors are unsettled by such stories and avoid the stock.

Also keep in mind that brokers and money managers are reluctant to tell bad stories to their clients. First, there is a pretty good chance that the client will reject the stock out of hand. Second, if the stock indeed does poorly, then the client has something to hold against the broker or money manager. "My broker told me it was a stock with a bad story, and indeed the stock performed poorly. Why did he have me buy it?" This is of particular concern when everyone else is recommending against the stock, a situation that is not uncommon with low PE stocks.

As a result, personal money managers stay away from bad story stocks as a way to avoid problems in dealing with their clients.

Value among Neglected Stocks

By definition, the vast sums managed by institutional investors are not directed at neglected stocks. Consequently price adjustment to new information is not as rapid for such stocks as it is for those stocks popular with institutions. This represents fertile hunting grounds for value investing.

Growth and Profitability

You might have found the previous discussion about small, low PE, neglected stocks a bit unsettling because these three characteristics are not the traditional ones used for identifying high potential stocks. In fact, the idea of investing in low PE (bad story) stocks or in stocks simply because they are neglected goes against most investor's better judgment.

On the contrary, investors intuitively feel that firms characterized by strong growth and profitability are better candidates for inclusion in their portfolio. But unlike small size, low PE and neglect, we have no proof that picking stocks based on growth and profitability enhances portfolio returns. If anything, it is the opposite: Portfolios comprised of such stocks on average underperform the market because such stocks have good stories that are easy to sell to investors, both individual and institutional. It is not uncommon for such stocks to be overvalued as the result of the huge sums of money rushing into them. Consequently, high growth and profitability stocks tend to have low upside potential along with large downside risk!

Despite this, you may still be interested in selecting stocks based on growth and profitability. You are thinking, rightfully so, that growth and profitability are the primary drivers of stock prices. So ignoring these two measures seems foolish indeed.

Adding a Secondary Screen

To get the best of both worlds, I suggest that you use growth and profitability as secondary screens after screening for size, PE and neglect. This will reduce the chance that you will overpay for the stock. As an example of this two-stage process, Figure 3.2 ranks by five-year earnings growth and return on equity (ROE) the NYSE companies listed in Figure 3.1. Recall that the NYSE companies in Figure 3.1 are among the smallest 20 percent in terms of size and neglect along with having a PE of less than 10.

If you want to focus on growth, you can limit yourself to the first six or seven stocks in the upper part of Figure 3.2. But if you want to focus on profitability, you can focus on the first six or seven stocks at the bottom of Figure 3.2. To focus on both growth and profitability, you need to choose some combination of the growth and profitability rankings in Figure 3.2.

Additional Secondary Screens on Risk

As is often said, where you find extra return, you will find extra risk. It therefore seems sensible to examine the riskiness of the stocks you are considering for your portfolio. But in Chapter 1, we noted how important it is to diversify properly through stock, industry, international and time diversification. The primary benefit of diversifying is that you reduce risk at the portfolio level. Concentrating on the riskiness of an individual stock, then, may be misleading because much of the individual stock risk will disappear inside the portfolio.

FIGURE 3.2 Small, Low PE and Neglected NYSE Stocks Ranked by Growth and ROE

Company	Ranked by 5-yr. Growth EPS (Annual %)
Oriental Bank & Trust	224
Westbridge Capital Corp.	97
Scott's Liquid Gold	77
The Sherwood Group, Inc.	30
Rowe Furniture Corp.	27
Aeroflex, Inc.	17
DDL Electronics, Inc.	15
Raytech Corporation	15
Boston Celtics L.P.	15
Chesapeake Utilities	2
CRI Liquidating REIT	–4
Asset Investors Corp.	–9
Great Northern Iron Ore	–12

Company	Ranked by ROE
Boston Celtics L.P.	132.7
Raytech Corporation	79.9
Great Northern Iron Ore	55.5
Rowe Furniture Corp.	22.7
The Sherwood Group, Inc.	22.1
Scott's Liquid Gold	18.8
Oriental Bank & Trust	17.4
Chesapeake Utilities	15.9
Aeroflex, Inc.	13.7
Asset Investors Corp.	11.8
CRI Liquidating REIT	10.8
Westbridge Capital Corp.	10.4
DDL Electronics, Inc.	–73.6

Source: *AAII Stock Investor,* January 31, 1996. Used with permission.

Another Look at Diversification and Risk

How is it that individual stock risk disappears inside a portfolio? First of all, risk disappears inside the portfolio only if you focus on *portfolio* risk rather than on *individual stock* risk. This may seem obvious, but many investors find it difficult to ignore the movement of individual stocks even when intellectually they know that overall portfolio performance is what counts.

Think of diversifying in terms of the economy as a whole. The economy has grown fairly consistently over the past 200 years or so. On the contrary, individual companies grow much more unpredictably. In fact, very few companies that existed 100 years ago are even around today. So a diversified portfolio acts more like the economy, growing predictably while individual stocks follow a more higgledy-piggledy pattern as individual industries and companies rise and fall in the chaos that is the Darwinian marketplace.

Beyond industry and firm diversification, time diversification also reduces risk. The chance you will lose money in the stock market on a daily basis is about 50 percent, while it is about 30 percent on an annual basis and drops to near zero over a 20-year period. For long time periods there is a very strong link between economic performance and stock market returns, while noise plays a dominant role on a daily basis. Because the economy has performed well over time, the chance of losing money in the stock market over long periods is nearly zero.

Adding a Secondary Risk Screen

Despite these diversification benefits, you may want to include risk as one of your screens in selecting individual stocks. Again, I would recommend using risk measures as a secondary screen after first screening for size, PE and neglect.

FIGURE 3.3 Small, Low PE and Neglected NYSE Stocks Ranked by Beta

Company	Ranked by Beta
Oriental Bank & Trust	0.27
Raytech Corporation	0.38
Great Northern Iron Ore	0.39
Boston Celtics L.P.	0.49
CRI Liquidating REIT	0.49
Rowe Furniture Corp.	0.52
Aeroflex, Inc.	0.60
Torch Energy Royalty Trust	0.61
Chesapeake Utilities	0.64
Westbridge Capital Corp.	0.76
DDL Electronics, Inc.	1.03
Asset Investors Corp.	1.27
The Sherwood Group, Inc.	2.06

Source: *AAII Stock Investor*, January 31, 1996. Used with permission.

Figure 3.3 shows a risk ranking based on beta, from low to high, for the NYSE stocks in Figure 3.1. *Beta* measures the relative volatility of the stock: A value greater than one signifies greater risk than the market; a value of less than one signifies less risk. Limit yourself to those stocks in the upper portion of Figure 3.3 as a way to reduce risk.

THE MECHANICS OF SCREENING

VALUE INVESTING TIPS

▼ If you use a home computer for screening, you can load many sources onto it or use one of several online information services.

▼ If you have no computer, you can use several services that provide screening information about large stock universes.

▼ Regardless of which way you go, size, PE and neglect should play a prominent role in your screening criteria.

In the first two sections of this chapter I argued that you should select your investment ideas from a very large universe and use screens based on size, PE and neglect to reduce the number of stocks to a manageable number. How do you actually go about doing this? You can use one of two general methods: computer and noncomputer.

To Use or Not To Use a Computer

Is it necessary to use a computer to screen and conduct a value analysis? The answer is no. If you do not use a computer, you will conduct your analysis in a different way, relying more on newspaper and magazine articles and will conduct a simpler set of hand calculations on each stock chosen for further analysis. If you use a computer, you will be able to process a larger database and will use software packages for screening and performing a larger number of calculations for each stock.

Is there an advantage to using a computer in value investing? In terms of portfolio performance, I do not believe so. The computer does perform many of the tedious steps of value investing with great speed, but regardless of whether or not you use one, a significant portion of value investing cannot be done on the computer. The critical steps of synthesizing the large amount of information about each stock and then deciding whether or not to buy or sell the stock require a considerable amount of judgment by you. Seldom is there a crystal clear buy or sell signal. Thus, whether or not you use a computer, you will be limited to analyzing no more than a half a dozen new stocks at a time (unless you love this stuff so much that you manage your portfolio full-time). Finally, keep in mind that your average holding period is three to five years, a time period over which the blinding analytic speed of the computer makes little or no difference.

Screening by Using a Computer

When you use a computer, you can automate a number of the tedious steps in value investing. This includes the screening step that you can conduct on a huge universe of stocks. For example, the *American Association of Individual Investors (AAII) Stock Investor* database contains nearly 7,000 stocks for which there are hundreds of data items for each stock. You can load this database onto your home computer, assuming it is fast and large enough.

Besides the many stock universes that you can load on your own computer, a number of online services allow you to screen and download current data to your computer. This approach has the advantage of the universe always being up-to-date, but in turn you have to pay for each minute of connect time.

Creating Your Screens

Once you have decided upon the source of stock data, you can set up your screens. This will require some trial and error on your part. As you test various screens, you will find some combination that works best for you. No matter which screen you decide upon, size, PE and neglect should play a central role.

The screens you use will change over time as market and economic conditions change. You will find that as the economy moves through a business cycle, different industries become undervalued and overvalued. Thus you may have to change your screens to avoid excessive concentration in a particular industry.

After you have selected the half dozen or so stocks that you wish to analyze further, you may need to import the data file into a spreadsheet program such as Excel, Lotus 1-2-3, etc. This will allow you maximum flexibility in conducting the rest of your value analysis.

Screening Without a Computer

If you do not use a computer for screening, you will have to keep your screening criteria in mind as you do your investment reading and research. Suggestions by your broker, companies you read or hear about and ideas that otherwise come to your attention will have to pass your screen before you proceed further with a detailed analysis. Size, PE and neglect should always play an important role in your screening.

Value Line, S&P, Investor's Business Daily and the *American Association of Individual Investors (AAII)* provide screening information for you. These services have the advantage of being based on a large universe of stocks. You will have to gain an understanding of the screening criteria used by each service and modify the criteria if necessary because their screening criteria may not exactly match your criteria. But the advantage of choosing from a large stock universe is enough to offset the disadvantage of having to modify the screening criteria.

Be True to Your Screening Criteria

By not using a computer, you will have to work a bit harder to ensure that you are selecting your stock ideas from a large universe and that you base your screening criteria on size, PE and neglect. It is very easy without a computer to become overwhelmed with the huge potential number of stocks and simply throw up your hands in despair. By doing so, you have effectively turned over a critical aspect of your portfolio to someone else (remember your broker, your barber, your brother?). So fight this urge and develop a screening technique that works for you.

▼ ▼ ▼

CHAPTER 4

Understanding Value Investing

VALUE INVESTOR'S CHECKLIST

✓ Through value investing, you are trying to identify those stocks that are currently mispriced by the market.

✓ One of the consequences of value investing is that you will invest in stocks with a wide range of future prospects but whose common feature is undervaluation.

✓ In growth investing, on the other hand, you are trying to identify the growth companies of the future, such as the next Microsoft or Netscape.

✓ Value analysis is not a precise science; the best you can hope for is to identify a value range for the stock and not a specific value per se.

✓ You can estimate the value range using a plethora of techniques based on dividends, earnings, cash flows and other financial series.

✓ You should sell overvalued stocks and avoid using the purchase price in your selling rules.

✓ Patience and humility are the keys to value investing.

✓ If you persevere with value investing, you can potentially outperform the market return by 2 percent to 3 percent over the long run (i.e., 12 percent to 13 percent annual return versus 10 percent for the market).

IDENTIFYING UNDERVALUED STOCKS

VALUE INVESTING TIPS

▼ The goal of value analysis is to identify undervalued stocks.

▼ In contrast, growth investing has as its goal the identification of the growth companies of the future.

▼ Value analysis begins with a look at the economy followed by a thorough exploration of the industry and the company.

▼ You spend most of your analysis time at the company level because this is where you have the best chance of enhancing your portfolio's return.

The basic goal of value investing is to identify undervalued stocks to include in your portfolio. You have already started along this path by screening the stock universe based on size, PE and neglect (see Chapter 3). Having identified a half dozen or so stocks for further analysis, you are now ready to plunge into the detailed world of value analysis.

Before you start, though, you need to have a solid understanding of what you are trying to accomplish in value investing. In particular, it is important that you appreciate the difference between value investing and growth investing.

Growth Investing

Growth investing is the most popular investment style among individual and institutional investors alike. Growth investing involves the search for those companies that will be successful in an ever-changing commercial marketplace. Most investors find this to be an appealing and exciting experience. Investing in the likes of Microsoft or Netscape before the rest of the world discovers them is exhilarating. Beyond this, most investors find it comforting to have successful company names in their portfolio.

Growth investing is also very appealing from the standpoint that a good story is much easier to sell than a bad story. Brokers and personal money managers alike are much more comfortable calling a client with a story about a company that is growing rapidly and has a bright future. Such stories sell well even though the idea of undervaluation or overvaluation is almost never mentioned. Tell a good enough story and investors will buy even the most overvalued stock.

In fact, growth stocks are what a dynamic economy is all about. Companies with innovative products and services that meet the constantly changing demands of consumers thrive in our market-driven economy. So it is only natural to want to identify these success stories ahead of time and invest in them. And if the stock market were completely rational all the time, then growth investing would be the only game in town.

Market Overreaction to Good News

But the market is not always rational. In reality, when the market gets excited about a stock, it often gets too excited. For example, at one point, Netscape, a company with $64 million in estimated 1995 sales and negligible earnings, had a market value of $6.5 billion! This was over 400 times book value and exceeded the market values of companies such as Corning, Mattel and Ralston Purina. Now it may turn out that Netscape and the Internet, on which it depends, will be phenomenally successful. But to justify this valuation, absolutely everything has to work out perfectly. Is it rational for the market to price a stock based on such a fairy-tale-like ending?

Market Overreaction to Bad News

On the other side of the value coin, the market often overreacts to bad news. In 1994, IBM was selling for as low as ten times earnings. It is true that IBM had lost money the two previous years, but a PE as low as ten implies virtually no growth for Big Blue. Was this a reasonable expectation? As it turns out, it was not because IBM has recovered from its recent problems.

The market overreaction in the IBM case is not an isolated incident. As we saw in Chapter 3, one of the best-performing segments of the market are those stocks with negative PEs, that is, those companies that have lost money over the previous year. The overreaction to bad news is a pervasive market characteristic.

Market Overreaction: The Basis for Value Investing

In a nutshell, Netscape and IBM provide concise allegories for the extreme mistakes made by the market: Investors collectively get too excited about the companies of the future and too quickly dump problem companies. This is where value investing garners its competitive advantage. By focusing on those areas where the market makes valuation mistakes instead of trying to identify the future economic success stories, value investors are able to deftly outmaneuver growth investors.

Economic Analysis: The Initial Step

Your detailed value analysis (see Figure 4.1) begins with a look at the economy. You will try to answer such questions as what is the current strength of the economy, what is the outlook for employment and inflation, and where is the economy in terms of the business cycle. Increasingly, the current state of the world economy has a major impact on the state of the U.S. economy. Although the economy is the starting point, it is not the most important part of value analysis. That distinction is reserved for company analysis. Your goal should be to learn enough about the economy to have a general understanding of its strength and outlook as a precursor to industry and company analysis.

Industry Analysis: The Second Step

Your next step involves an industry analysis in which you will take a fairly detailed look at the industry of interest. You may have identified this particular industry as a by-product of the screening process described in Chapter 3, or you may have decided to focus your analysis at the industry level rather than at the company level. There is no right or wrong answer to which way is best. Regardless, a thorough analysis of the industry is an important feature of value investing.

Company Analysis: The Critical Step

The final and most important step is a company analysis. Here you will look at the market position of the company as well as its financial strength,

FIGURE 4.1 An Overview of Value Analysis

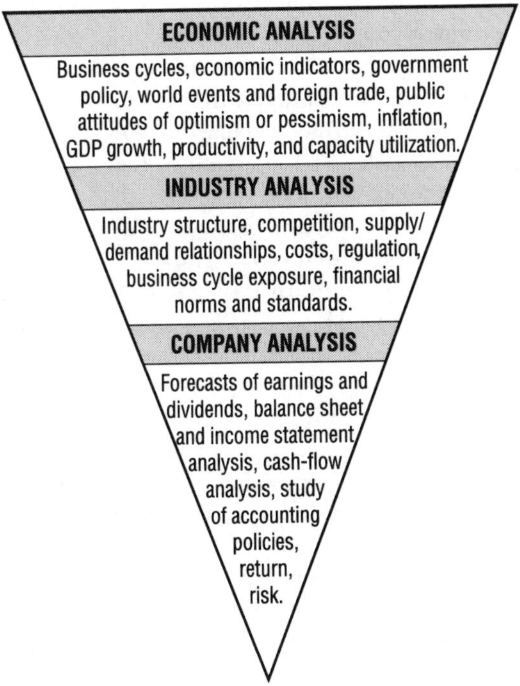

ECONOMIC ANALYSIS
Business cycles, economic indicators, government policy, world events and foreign trade, public attitudes of optimism or pessimism, inflation, GDP growth, productivity, and capacity utilization.

INDUSTRY ANALYSIS
Industry structure, competition, supply/demand relationships, costs, regulation, business cycle exposure, financial norms and standards.

COMPANY ANALYSIS
Forecasts of earnings and dividends, balance sheet and income statement analysis, cash-flow analysis, study of accounting policies, return, risk.

Source: *AAII Stock Analysis Workbook.* Used with permission.

profitability and future growth prospects. You will attempt to identify both the strengths and weaknesses of the company. Since you started with a series of screens that are based on size, PE and neglect, you can be fairly sure that you will uncover a number of weaknesses.

Your task is to synthesize both the positive and negative information about the company and determine whether or not the company is undervalued. Again, keep in mind that at this stage, a fair amount of art is incorporated in the science of value investing.

Why Focus on Company Analysis?

The emphasis on the company rather than on the economy is at odds with studies showing that the primary long-term driver of portfolio return is the long-term performance of the economy. Very little if any of portfolio performance can be attributed to the investment manager's ability to pick individual stocks. So why spend so much time on company analysis?

The answer goes back to the issue of where you as an investor can enhance return. The evidence clearly shows that information about the economy is rapidly reflected in stock prices. In fact, as we will see in more detail in Chapter 5, the stock market itself is one of the best forecasters of future economic activity, leading the economy by an average of six months. Since the chances of enhancing your portfolio return by focusing on the economy seem remote, why spend any more time on this part of the analysis than you need to gain a general understanding of the economy?

On the contrary, there is ample evidence, much of which I have already described, showing that company-specific information is not always rapidly reflected in stock prices. Only the staunchest believer in informationally efficient markets could accept the notion that every piece of information about the thousands of individual stocks traded on the many exchanges is accurately reflected in the prices of each and every stock. Stock analysts, the primary engine behind stock price changes, are a limited resource. So prices will be correct only to the extent that analyst time and effort are available to process the torrent of new of information. Consequently, individual stocks represent a fertile field in which you can sow your analytical efforts.

ESTIMATING A VALUE RANGE

VALUE INVESTING TIPS

▼ The value range allows you to separate the buy and sell signals from the background of noisy company information.

▼ The primary source of fundamental value is the stream of current and future dividends paid by the company.

▼ As a way to estimate the company's ability to pay dividends, you will focus on dividends, earnings, cash flow and, at times, revenues, book value and assets.

▼ You will find it necessary to estimate value multipliers for each financial series used.

One of the important final products of a company analysis is the determination of a value range, the price range that is consistent with the company's fundamentals, such as dividends, earnings, cash flow and revenues. If the stock price is below the value range, then the stock is undervalued and it is a buy candidate. On the other hand, if the stock price is above this value range, then it is overvalued and a sell candidate. A stock with a price falling within the value range is said to be properly valued.

Separating the Signal from the Noise

The width of the value range reflects the difficulty of estimating a precise value due to the noisiness of company information. In essence by estimating a value range, you are trying to sift out the signal from the noise. The basic idea is that if the stock price deviates far enough from its fundamen-

FIGURE 4.2   Value Range Versus Price for a Stock

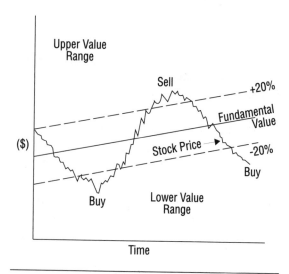

Source: *AAII Stock Analysis Workbook.* Used with permission.

tal value, then there is a good chance that market forces will bring the price back towards a correct valuation. Small deviations from fundamental value, the noisy price movements captured within the value range, are not large enough to trigger such market forces. Therefore, the width of the value range represents the stock's noise band.

Figure 4.2 shows a value range for a hypothetical stock. The central line represents the best estimate of the company's *fundamental value*, the maximum price you would be willing to pay for the stock, which is bracketed in Figure 4.2 by a value range of ±20 percent. The actual stock price meanders through this range, at times rising above the range and at times falling below it. These are the times of greatest interest to you, either to buy or to sell the stock. Both a buy and a sell signal are shown in Figure 4.2.

The value range of ±20 percent in Figure 4.2 is about as narrow a range as you will be able to estimate. The information about a particular stock, such as revenues, earnings, cash flow and to a lesser extent dividends, are very noisy in their own right. Noise-inducing events include bad weather that temporarily reduces revenues, a single product success that increases earnings and a change in accounting treatment that alters cash flow. Because literally hundreds of such events each year impact the financial information for a company, determining what is a fundamental change and what is simply noise is very difficult.

The Value Range Widens with an Increase in Noise

The ±20 percent value range in Figure 4.2 might be for utilities and blue chip companies for which information is readily available and is less noisy. As you consider more growth-oriented companies, information gets harder to find and is much noisier. Consequently, the value range widens to perhaps ±30 percent or ±40 percent. If you are considering smaller growth stocks traded on the Nasdaq, your value range might even widen to ±50 percent or ±60 percent.

If you go to the extreme of investing in companies with little or no financial history, you might not be able to estimate a value range at all. Such companies include any initial public offering (IPO) with little or no operating history. The width of the value range you use is dictated by the noisiness of the company's information, tempered by your own judgment.

The Value Range Is Central

Keep in mind that factors beyond the value range will enter into your decision to buy or sell the stock. While the value range plays a central role in value investing, always make your buy and sell decision in the context of other quantitative and qualitative aspects of the company. Most of the time you will gather and analyze a great deal of information about the company (known as *due diligence* in the investment business). Make your decisions the result of a carefully crafted mosaic based on all available information, with the value range as a central feature.

Dividends Are Primary

The primary source of stock value is the dividends paid to shareholders. *Dividends per share* (DPS) represent the cash return for putting money at risk with a company. Put another way, the fundamental value of a stock is the present value of the current and future dividend stream. In a bottom line sense, nothing but dividends matter. Thinking about stock valuation in this way is identical to the way in which you think about other investment opportunities: Is the current and future cash stream from this investment worth the initial price you are paying?

But for many stocks, current dividends per share represent only a small portion of the *total return* (dividends plus capital gains). Indeed, many stocks pay no dividends at all, ranging from 37 percent of NYSE stocks paying dividends down to only 3 percent of over-the-counter stocks (OTC). Even for the NYSE, the average dividend yield is a mere 2.5 percent out of a long-term total return of around 10 percent.

Why Invest in Zero-Dividend Stocks?

If DPS is the primary source of fundamental value, then why should you bother with all those dividendless stocks? In fact, this is how some investors think, and they indeed limit their investments to dividend-paying stocks. As a side comment, if you lived in Germany, this would characterize the typical investor.

But here in the United States, the vast majority of stock investors are willing to consider zero-dividend stocks. Where is the source of value for these stocks? In theory, shareholders have full claim on the earnings of the company even though management may be retaining everything for reinvestment purposes. By allowing management to do this, shareholders are hoping the retained earnings will be reinvested in profitable opportunities so that when the company actually begins paying dividends, they will be very large indeed. Obviously this requires a great deal of optimism on the part of shareholders. This may explain why U.S. investors are willing to invest in such companies while their German counterparts are not.

Thus earnings represent a proxy for the company's future ability to pay dividends. Larger earnings imply that the company's future dividend potential is greater. Again, the fundamental source of value is the stream of current and future dividends.

Estimating Fundamental Value

The two most popular financial series for estimating fundamental value are DPS and *earnings per share* (EPS). The argument for using DPS is obvious. The argument for using EPS even for dividend-paying companies is that dividends, both present and future, spring forth from current EPS. Management pays current dividends from current earnings and retains the remainder to fund future growth in revenues, earnings and eventually future growth in dividends. For this reason, many analysts feel that current EPS is in some sense more "fundamental" than is current DPS.

Using Cash Flow per Share for Estimating Value

Another popular series for measuring fundamental value is *cash flow per share*. It is estimated by adding depreciation and other noncash items (generally insignificant for most companies) back to EPS. Depreciation as well as other noncash items are important for estimating taxes but do not represent a cash outlay for the company. Thus some analysts feel that cash flow per share is a better measure than is EPS.

Another variation is known as *net free cash flow per share* and is estimated by subtracting capital outlays from cash flow. Some analysts feel that net free cash flow is a superior measure of the sustainable fundamental cash flow of the company because it nets out the money spent to maintain the assets of the company.

These four measures of the company's ability to pay current and future dividends are the primary series used for estimating fundamental value. You will find it helpful to know how to use each of these series in identifying undervalued stocks. In some cases, you will emphasize one series over the others; in other situations, you will use some combination of all four. The vast majority of stocks can be valued using one or some combination of these four series.

Value Multipliers

In a few situations, however, you may have to estimate value based on other series such as revenues, book value or assets. Usually this involves smaller companies with very little financial history and which have not as yet become profitable, such as many IPOs.

Regardless of which financial series you use, you will have to estimate a *value multiplier* (VM). The VM is the number used to transform the series into a value estimate. For example, if DPS is $1 and the VM for dividends is 25, your value estimate is $25. The VM will differ for each series used. (See Chapter 7 for more on a number of VM estimation techniques.)

Estimating a Value Range

Transforming DPS, EPS, cash flow per share, net free cash flow per share and perhaps other series by means of a VM will result in a range of values. Even if you limit the value estimation to a single series, you will end up with a value range. This latter range results from a variety of series estimates (i.e., several estimates of EPS) and/or a variety of VMs (i.e., several estimates of PE, maybe high, average and low for the year). By pulling all these value estimates together and mixing in a fair amount of personal judgment, you will end up with a value range for the stock. Again, the noisier the financial series used, the wider will be the value range.

Determining Undervaluation and Overvaluation

If price falls within the value range, then you conclude that the stock is fairly priced within the precision of the information and the valuation techniques that you have used. If it falls below the range, you conclude that the stock is undervalued and a buy candidate. If the stock price is above the value range, then you conclude the stock is overvalued and a sell candidate. If you have conducted a careful analysis, you cannot attribute the undervaluation or overvaluation to the vagaries of the data. You have captured this in the width of the value range.

THE ART OF SELLING

VALUE INVESTING TIPS

▼ Quite often emotion dominates the selling decision because your wealth goes up and down as the stock price gyrates.

▼ Look forward when making the sell decision rather than backward at the price you paid for the stock.

▼ Follow the basic rule of selling overvalued stocks by focusing on the current price and the value range.

Much of the focus in this book is on buying stocks. But that is only half the story. Once you purchase a stock, you then need to decide when to sell it. The banal rule of "buy low, sell high" doesn't help much. In fact, trying to follow it may very well lead to poor long-term performance.

So what rule do you follow when selling a stock? The answer is really quite simple: Sell the stock if it is overvalued. The execution of this simple rule is, however, much more problematic. When buying a stock, convincing yourself to stick with undervalued stocks is fairly easy, but when selling, it is very easy to be driven by emotions instead.

The Hard-Nosed Buyer and the Emotional Seller

Are these two separate people? In my experience, including with my own portfolio, both descriptions apply to most stock investors. While you can be hard nosed when picking among the many stocks available for purchase, it is very difficult to be as dispassionate when it is your own money! Once you purchase a stock, it almost becomes a member of the family. And you may start treating it like one. You might begin to take price movements personally and say to yourself, "How dare that stock price go down! Doesn't it know that I am counting on it to go up?"

Another problem unique to selling is that, unlike the purchase decision that focuses only on the stock price at the time of purchase, the owner of a stock follows every up and down of the price. It is *your* wealth going up and down not just some abstract notion of volatility. You come to believe that you are a helpless victim on the market roller coaster.

Emotional Selling Rules

It is no wonder that many investors turn to a new set of rules for the sell decision. Such rules include "I will sell this stock when it has gone up 20 percent," "I will sell this stock when it has gone down 10 percent," or "I will sell this stock if it doesn't change much over the next two years," or my favorite, "I will sell this stock when it gets back up to the price I paid for it!"

This latter rule plays a major role for many investors. It is only human to convince yourself that if you *don't* sell the stock, you have *not* lost money. But this represents a very poor decision rule. Where is the hard-nosed analysis of price and value in this rule? Instead, you need to remove your emotions from the sell decision. If it makes sense to sell the stock (i.e., if it is overvalued), then accept the loss. Remember that you don't want money invested in overvalued stocks because the future return potential for such stocks is poor.

Look Forward Not Backward

You might object to the advice of selling a stock for a loss because this does not seem to be consistent with the goal of value investing. But keep in mind that value investing is a forward-looking process. You always strive to invest your money for the best possible future return. Looking backward at the price you paid for the stock does not help you in this process. That is, the price you paid for the stock is irrelevant in making current investment decisions.

Accepting Your Mistakes and Moving On

This is so hard for many investors to do that I have often thought about developing a 12-step program to help investors forget the past when selling stocks. Step 1 of this program would be: "I admit that I have *lost* money in this stock even though I have *not* sold it." Like many other serious maladies, admitting that you have a problem with selling losing stocks is the first step toward recovery.

You would be surprised how many people can't admit this. Or maybe you aren't so surprised because you can't admit it yourself. By the way, in case you are curious, I have yet to work out the other 11 steps in the stock seller's 12-step program.

Portfolio Performance Counts

So looking backward at actual performance is not the way to make a sell decision. The fact is that as you buy and sell stocks, you will make money on some, lose money on some and break even on others. Again long-term *portfolio* performance counts, not individual stock performance. By pursuing value investing, you are setting your sails in order to profit from the market's tendency to make valuation mistakes. Every stock you purchase will not be a winner, but your overall portfolio will be.

The bottom line is that only two things matter in selling stocks: the *current* stock price and the value range. If the stock is overvalued, then sell it. Period. Strive to be as hard nosed about selling as you are about buying. And always look forward and not backward.

PATIENCE AND HUMILITY: THE WATCHWORDS OF VALUE INVESTING

VALUE INVESTING TIPS

▼ No matter how much you learn about value investing, you will never get to the point of complete control over your portfolio.

▼ If you stick with the techniques of value investing, you can expect a 2 percent to 3 percent improvement in portfolio return.

▼ In the short run, you will be able to select a winning stock about 55 percent of the time.

▼ Value investing goes through dry spells, so it is important that you persevere and not abandon the technique during these tough times.

The next few chapters describe in detail the dozens of techniques that collectively represent the heart and soul of value investing. As you dig through this material, do not lose the forest for the trees. No matter how much you learn about value investing or how carefully you apply the techniques, you still will not be able to catch speeding bullets or to jump over tall buildings.

Remain Patient and Humble

In pursuing value investing, you are improving the chances of building a winning portfolio. But there will continue to be considerable noise in the stock market and in the movements of individual stocks. And you will never get to the point where your decisions work out all of the time or even a vast majority of the time. Patience is crucial.

Beyond being patient, do not overestimate your stock picking ability lest the market remind you who is more powerful. Don't be like the people who continued to buy the "nifty-fifty" (about 50 large growth stocks that were thought to be sure winners) in the early 1970s even after the average PE ratio topped 30, then watched as their portfolios plummeted in value, not fully recovering until 1982. Maintain a healthy respect for the market along with being humble about your own stock picking abilities.

Setting Long-Term Performance Expectations

What are reasonable expectations for your winning portfolio? I have already pointed out that the vast majority of professional managers underperform the market, so to exceed the market return is no easy task. But if you don't, then why spend the time on value investing?

A reasonable long-term goal for your portfolio is to beat the market by 2 percent to 3 percent (i.e., 12 percent to 13 percent average return compared to the market average of 10 percent). Now this may not seem like much, and for short time periods, it is not. But for longer time periods, the benefit is substantial.

Figure 4.3 shows the gains in portfolio value resulting from outperforming the market by 2 percent or 3 percent annually over periods ranging from 10 to 40 years. For a 40-year time period and a 3 percent extra return, the difference is a dramatic 129 percent, which means that value investing would produce a portfolio worth more than twice the one resulting from simply investing in a market index. Almost everyone would agree that this gain is worth the extra effort required by value investing. You may not have this long a time frame, but value investing produces substantial gains over shorter periods as well, as Figure 4.3 shows.

FIGURE 4.3 Potential Gains to Value Investing*

Time Period in Years	Percent Increase in Ending Portfolio Value when Portfolio Earns an Extra:	
	2% per Year	3% per Year
10	10%	16%
20	26	41
30	47	78
40	73	129

*Assumes equal dollar additions to portfolio each year and an average 10% stock market return.

The Basis for Superior Performance

What is the basis for this estimate of 2 percent to 3 percent extra return? This estimate, based on my own research and the research of others, is about as good as you can hope for. What about all those investment managers' claims that they are constantly clobbering the market return? Few of these claims survive when they are held up to the light of day. Typically their portfolios have performed well over a short time period, but when examined over a longer period, their performance is average or below. Studies using comparable time periods for every manager show little evidence of superior performance. So the best you can reasonably hope for is an extra 2 percent to 3 percent.

Short-Term Performance Expectations

So much for the long run, how about the short term? If you are beating the market by 2 percent to 3 percent over the long run, what will you observe with your individual stock selections? You will be selecting stocks that beat the market return about 55 percent of the time. This means that 45 percent of your stock selections will underperform the market. Now this is humbling.

This 55 percent does not seem like much, but it is enough to produce the 2 percent to 3 percent long-term advantage. And it is only a bit better than 50/50, which brings home, in the starkest terms, the need for you to remain patient and humble.

An Example

If you have a portfolio composed of, say, 15 stocks and are aiming for a three-year to five-year average holding period, you will sell on average three of your current stocks a year and correspondingly buy three new stocks. With such small numbers and a 55 percent chance of success, you have a good chance that in any one year all of the stocks you purchased will do poorly (of course, it is even more likely that all of them will do very well, but for some reason this outcome doesn't test your patience as much).

Sticking with Value Investing

How long will you stick with a technique that doesn't seem to work? One year? Two years? Five years? My experience shows that many investors hang on for a year or two but will bail out shortly thereafter if things don't improve. The stark reality is that every technique that seems to work, from size to PE to neglect to value investing, has dry spells that can last up to five years in length. This span is well beyond most investors' natural level of patience, so many bail out and thus hurt their long-term performance.

Now I know what you are thinking: "Can't I just temporarily abandon value investing and come back when it starts working again?" The answer is no because there seems to be no way to predict when value investing will start and stop working. So you have to be patient and tough it out during dry spells. Just avoid your portfolio as a topic of conversation at cocktail parties during these sluggish periods.

CHAPTER 5

▼ ▼ ▼

Examining Economic Forces Affecting the Market

VALUE INVESTOR'S CHECKLIST

✓ Over the long run, the most important force behind the market is the economy; the U.S. stock market has done well because the U.S. economy has done well.

✓ Over shorter periods of time, however, the link between the economy and the market is much weaker.

✓ As the U.S. economy has increased in size and has grown more interdependent with otherworld economies, the ability of the U.S. government to control economic activity has diminished.

✓ Even the ability of the Federal Reserve to dampen economic cycles through control of the money supply seems to have diminished in recent years.

✓ For investors, the most important aspect of monetary policy is the risk of inflation.

✓ In terms of value investing, the most important economic tendencies are undervaluation at business cycle troughs and overvaluation at business cycle peaks.

ECONOMIC DRIVERS OF THE MARKET

VALUE INVESTING TIPS

▼ Over the past 200 years, the long-term real (i.e., net of inflation) stock return has averaged 6 percent, twice the average annual real growth rate for Gross Domestic Product (GDP).

▼ The relationship in which the real stock return is roughly double the real GDP growth rate seems to hold for countries other than the United States.

▼ Daily market price changes are dominated by noise and have little or no relationship to economic fundamentals.

▼ Annual market price changes are about 50 percent noise while the remaining 50 percent is explained equally by six-month-ahead economic changes and market-wide valuation measures such as yield and PE.

As you watch the market gyrate on a daily basis, it is hard to imagine that it has any fundamental relationship with the economy at all. But if you look at the market over a longer time period, the relationship between the market and the economy becomes profound. The stock market has done well over the long run because the economy has done well over the long run. Thus, investing in the stock

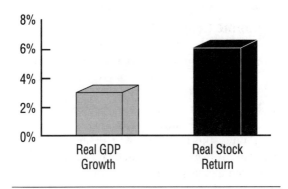

market is like casting a vote of confidence for the
long-term economic success of the United States.

The Long-Term Relationship Between
the Economy and the Stock Market

The long-term growth relationship between the
economy and the market is portrayed in Figure 5.1.
Gross Domestic Product (GDP) is the broadest measure
of the annual output of goods and services. You
might be more familiar with a concept called Gross
National Product (GNP) that in the past was used to
measure U.S. output. GDP is essentially the same
magnitude as GNP. GDP accounts for output on a
production facility location basis rather than on an
ownership basis as does GNP. For the United States,
GDP exceeds $7 trillion or more than $27,000 per
capita. By this latter measure, the United States
enjoys the highest standard of living in the world.

The GDP growth rate and market return
reported in Figure 5.1 are net of inflation or "real."
The sum of the market real return of 6 percent reported in Figure 5.1 and the 3 percent average
inflation rate experienced in recent years is roughly

equal to the long-term market nominal return of 10 percent that I use elsewhere in this book.

Why Are Stock Returns Double the Economic Growth Rate?

An obvious question that arises when studying Figure 5.1 is: Why is the market's real return double the real growth rate in GDP? On average, companies in the United States are financed about 50 percent with debt and about 50 percent with equity. Over time, the real return to debtholders, who invest in the firm's short-term financial instruments (e.g., commercial paper, banker's acceptances, etc.) and bonds, has averaged near zero. Thus the total real return to the average company (the direct consequence of the real growth in GDP) has been disproportionately allocated to shareholders as evidenced by the 6 percent average real stock return.

How does this allocation of real returns happen? Risk averse investors are attracted to short-term instruments and bonds. Over time, risk averse investors have collectively been content with receiving a near zero real return on these nearly risk-free debt instruments. The extra return not paid to debtholders is then passed to shareholders via the market pricing mechanism. Thus shareholders who take on the risk of owning stocks receive a higher real return. Aren't markets wonderful?

The Economy and Market Returns in Other Countries

The doubling of the real GDP growth rate shown in Figure 5.1 seems to hold roughly for countries other than the United States. But the difference is that in other countries, the real GDP growth can be much higher. China, for example, has grown at nearly a 10 percent rate over the last ten years. Thus a 20 percent average real stock return is entirely possible. This again is a strong reason for investing outside the United States because many countries have a growth potential exceeding that of the United States.

Daily Stock Price Changes

While the economy is the most important driver behind market returns over the long run, the relationship between the two over short time periods is much weaker. Hourly, daily, weekly, monthly and even annual market price changes often have little to do with underlying economic fundamentals. Instead, noise plays an increasingly important role as the time period is shortened. Price changes are considered noise if they occur for no obvious fundamental reason.

Virtually all daily price changes can be considered noise in that changes in economic and firm fundamentals explain very few daily price changes. But there is no lack of effort by traders, analysts, brokers and the media to link price changes with underlying fundamentals.

Example of the Power of Noise

"Dr. Howard, we would like to talk to you about what happened in the stock market today," said the news producer of a local TV station.

"What happened to the market?" I asked, caught a bit off guard.

"The market experienced one of its biggest drops in history. We would like to talk to you on the air about why it happened.," the producer replied.

"I have no idea why it happened," I said firmly.

"That's no problem, we will be there in an hour," came the equally firm reply, and the phone went dead.

I quickly dialed one of my friends in a local Denver investment firm and began to ask about the day's events. She told me that the market had indeed plummeted during the day and that the word on the street was that the decline was caused by rising interest rates and lower earnings forecasts for several big companies. Sure enough, in an hour, the TV cameras arrived, and I was being grilled by the news anchor.

"Dr. Howard, why do you think the market dropped today?" asked the news anchor.

"Well, thanks for asking me that question. I believe it is because interest rates are rising and earnings are down.," I said in my deepest and most authoritative voice!

I sounded very authoritative indeed!

Trying To Make Sense of Short-Term Price Movements

The truth is that there is probably no explanation for the market drop on that particular day. Some days the market goes up and some days it goes down, and there is no warning of which will happen. But you can't say that into the camera when it is pointed at you. So the story springs to life and becomes the conventional wisdom for that particular day. This scenario is played out thousands of times each day as anxious investors, brokers, reporters and others try to make sense out of the noisy spasms of the market.

Now you may have found the story quite plausible, for indeed when interest rates go up and earnings expectations go down, the stock market should indeed go down. But the real question is whether this relationship is consistent enough to explain daily price movements? The evidence says no. In reality, you can find other days with virtually the same information on interest rates and earnings when the price went up instead of down. There are too many pieces of information constantly flooding into the market to be able to identify any particular one of them as the cause of market movements. Many studies verify the futility of trying to make sense out of daily price changes.

FIGURE 5.2   Drivers of Annual Stock
              Price Changes

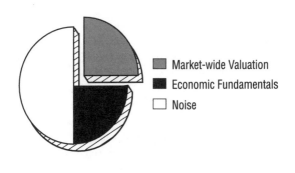

Market-wide Valuation
Economic Fundamentals
Noise

Annual Price Changes

A careful examination of annual price changes presents a picture that is somewhere between the noise-dominated daily price change picture and the economy-dominated long-term price change picture. In addition, evidence of a market-wide undervaluation to overvaluation cycle begins to emerge. Figure 5.2 shows the percent of annual stock price changes explained by each of three drivers: (1) market-wide valuation changes, (2) economic fundamentals and (3) noise.

Future Economic Changes

Figure 5.2 illustrates that changes in economic fundamentals (e.g., industrial production, GDP, etc.) explain 25 percent of annual stock price movements. It is not, however, changes in current fundamentals but changes in the economy six months, on average, from now. What is happening in the market today is partially in anticipation of what will be happening in the economy six months from now.

But this result shouldn't be too surprising. After all, economic performance is the basis for market performance, and so investors have a strong incentive to forecast economic activity as far into the future as possible. Apparently, six months is as far ahead as investors can forecast.

Still a Lot of Noise

Figure 5.2 shows that 50 percent of annual price changes remain unexplained and thus can be categorized as noise. Perhaps the techniques and information used to explain price movements will improve, and more price changes will be explained. But I am not very hopeful this will be the case. My own extensive research in this area leads me to believe that a large fraction of price changes will forever remain unexplained, even for annual data.

Market-wide Valuation Variables

The last category in Figure 5.2 represents the market-wide valuation variables. These include market dividend yield and market PE ratio, which explain about 25 percent of the annual price changes. Before discussing these valuation variables, we need to examine in the next section the impact of the business cycle on the market. The last section in this chapter deals with the market-wide valuation variables.

TRACKING THE BUSINESS CYCLE

VALUE INVESTING TIPS

▼ The average post-WWII business cycle lasted nearly five years and consisted of a one-year recession followed by a four-year expansion.

▼ However, business cycles are anything but regular; some last only 18 months and some last as long as 10 years.

▼ The Index of Leading Economic Indicators has the disadvantage of including stock prices as the most important of the 11 series making up the index.

▼ The Purchasing Managers Index has the best record for accurately representing the current state of the economy.

It is hard to imagine, but for the first 160 years of this country's existence, virtually no data was gathered about the workings of the U.S. economy. Can you imagine a world without data on GDP, employment, consumer prices and so forth? But since 1930, the government data mills have evolved to the point where they release new economic information on a daily basis. What should you keep track of out of this deluge of economic indicators?

Measuring Real GDP Growth

One of the best measures of economic activity is real annual GDP growth, which is reported in Figure 5.3 by quarters for 1994 and 1995. In Figure 5.3, you clearly see when the economy's performance exceeded or fell short of the stock market's long-term economic growth expectation of 3 percent. For example, 1995 was a year of economic underperformance, while 1994 was a year of strong performance.

You will notice the economic performance during these two years was opposite the performance of the market: 1994 was a poor year for the market while 1995 was a good year. This demonstrates the often weak short-term relationship between the economy and the market. (Interest rates were another major factor during these two years, with rates rising dramatically in 1994 and falling dramatically in 1995. In fact, these two years were quite exceptional with respect to interest rates.)

FIGURE 5.3   Growth Rates for Real Gross
                    Domestic Product

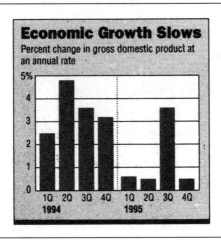

Recessions and Expansions

Figure 5.4 provides a comprehensive history of
U.S. business cycles. The second column details the
length in months for each of the 31 contractions
(i.e., recession or depression) that have occurred
since 1854. The third column lists the length of the
corresponding expansion. A trip down these two
columns reveals that the business cycle is anything
but regular. Contractions have lasted for as short a
time as six months or as long as five years (the
depression of 1873–79). On the other hand, expansions have persisted for as short as 12 months or as
long as nine years (the expansion of 1961–1969).
Despite their namesake, business cycles are not at
all regular.

Figure 5.4 reports at the bottom the average
post-WWII recession has lasted about one-year and
the average expansion has lasted nearly four years
resulting in an average full business cycle of nearly

five years. As we saw in Chapter 1, this five-year average length is why the holding period resulting from value investing averages from three to five years in length. The variability in the length of the business cycle is one reason why holding periods vary from stock to stock.

Where Are We in the Current Business Cycle?

How do you determine the current point in the business cycle? There are two indicators that are helpful.

The Index of Leading Economic Indicators.

This index (see Figure 5.5) is comprised of the 11 economic series that have the best record for predicting economic turning (i.e., peaks and troughs). The more accurate the economic series is in predicting, the more heavily it is weighted in calculating the index.

Unfortunately for stock investors, the most heavily weighted of the 11 component series is stock prices. Thus movements in the Index of Leading Economic Indicators are strongly influenced by movements in the stock market. This makes the index of marginal benefit for stock investors. The dramatic impact of stock prices was demonstrated in October 1987 when the stock market crashed and the index dropped precipitously. As a result, virtually everyone was predicting a recession or even a depression. Articles comparing 1987 to 1929 were commonplace. But the recession did not materialize, and in fact, the economy remained strong until 1990. The only segment of the economy that went into a recession was Wall Street!

Rather than focusing on the index as a whole, you need to focus on the ten other series besides stock prices. These ten indicators clearly represent new incremental information. They may also help forecast future economic activity in various segments of the economy, something that will be useful when you begin a detailed value analysis. The

FIGURE 5.4 Business Cycle Expansions and Contractions

Business Cycle Reference Dates

Trough	Peak
December 1854	June 1857 . . . .
December 1858	October 1860 . . . .
June 1861.	April 1865. . . . .
December 1867	June 1869 . . . .
December 1870	October 1873 . . . .
March 1879	March 1882. . . . .
May 1885	March 1887. . . . .
April 1888	July 1890. . . . .
May 1891	January 1893. . . . .
June 1894.	December 1895 . . . .
June 1897.	June 1899 . . . .
December 1900	September 1902 . . . .
August 1904.	May 1907 . . . .
June 1908.	January 1910. . . . .
January 1912	January 1913. . . . .
December 1914	August 1918 . . . .
March 1919	January 1920. . . . .
July 1921	May 1923 . . . .
July 1924	October 1926 . . . .
November 1927	August 1929 . . . .
March 1933	May 1937 . . . .
June 1938.	February 1945 . . . .
October 1945.	November 1948 . . . .
October 1949.	July 1953. . . . .
May 1954	August 1957 . . . .
April 1958	April 1960. . . . .
February 1961	December 1969 . . . .
November 1970	November 1973 . . . .
March 1975	January 1980. . . . .
July 1980	July 1981. . . . .
November 1982	July 1990. . . . .
March 1991	

Average, all cycles: . . . .
   1854-1991 (31 cycles). . . . .
   1854-1919 (16 cycles). . . . .
   1919-1945 (6 cycles). . . . .
   1945-1991 (9 cycles). . . . .

Average, peacetime cycles:
   1854-1991 (26 cycles). . . . .
   1854-1919 (14 cycles). . . . .
   1919-1945 (5 cycles). . . . .
   1945-1991 (7 cycles). . . . .

1. 30 cycles.
2. 15 cycles.
3. 25 cycles.
4. 13 cycles.

Source: *Survey of Current Business,* April 1995.

FIGURE 5.4 Business Cycle Expansions and Contributions *(Continued)*

Duration in Months

Contraction (Trough from Previous Peak)	Expansion (Trough to Peak)	Cycle Trough from Previous Trough	Peak from Previous Peak
—	30	—	—
18	22	48	40
8	*46*	30	*54*
32	18	*78*	50
18	34	36	52
65	36	99	101
38	22	74	60
13	27	35	40
10	20	37	30
17	18	37	35
18	24	36	42
18	21	42	39
23	33	44	56
13	19	46	32
24	12	43	36
23	*44*	35	*67*
7	10	*51*	17
18	22	28	40
14	27	36	41
13	21	40	34
43	50	64	*93*
13	*80*	63	93
8	37	*88*	45
11	*45*	48	*56*
10	39	*55*	49
8	24	47	32
10	*106*	34	*116*
11	36	*117*	47
16	58	52	74
6	12	64	18
16	92	28	108
8	—	100	—
18	35	53	53[1]
22	27	48	49[2]
18	35	53	53
11	50	61	61
19	29	48	48[3]
22	24	46	47[4]
20	26	46	45
11	43	53	53

Note: Figures printed in bold italic are the wartime expansions (Civil War, World Wars I and II, Korean war and Vietnam war), the postwar contractions, and the full cycles that include the wartime expansions.

Source: National Bureau of Economic Research, Inc., 1050 Massachusetts Avenue, Cambridge, MA 02138.

**FIGURE 5.5 Index of Leading Economic
Indicators**

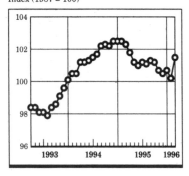

Leading Indicators

Index (1987 = 100)

Source: Reprinted by permission of *The Wall Street
Journal*, © 1996 Dow Jones & Company, Inc. All
Rights Reserved Worldwide.

Index of Leading Economic Indicators (in brief)

1. Average work week of manufacturing
    production workers
2. Initial claims for unemployment insurance
3. Change in consumer confidence
4. Price changes in sensitive crude materials
5. Contracts and orders for plant and equipment
6. Vendor performance
7. Stock prices
8. Money supply
9. New orders
10. Residential building permits
11. Factory backlogs of durable goods orders

changes in all 11 series are reported around the first
of each month in *Investor's Business Daily*.

The Purchasing Managers Index.   This
index (see Figure 5.6) is based on a survey of 300
members of the National Association of Purchasing
Managers who work in a wide range of industries,

FIGURE 5.6 Purchasing Managers Index

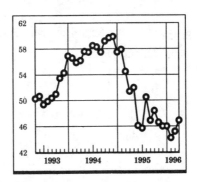

Purchasing Managers Index

Source: Reprinted by permission of *The Wall Street Journal,* © 1996 Dow Jones & Company, Inc. All Rights Reserved Worldwide.

primarily manufacturing. The results are released two weeks after the monthly survey is conducted and summarized as the percentage reporting strong business conditions for their particular firm in terms of employment, shipments, delivery times, prices and so forth. The index typically ranges between 40 percent and 60 percent, representing the percentage of those surveyed reporting favorable business conditions. This means that in the best of economic times, 60 percent of U.S. businesses are doing well, while in the worst of economic times, 40 percent of businesses are doing well.

The Purchasing Managers Index can be interpreted as follows:

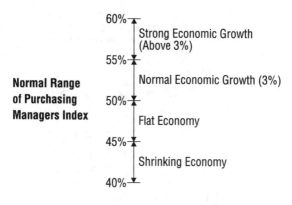

I have followed this index for 15 years, and unlike the Index of Leading Economic Indicators, I have yet to see a false signal emanate from the Purchasing Managers Index. For example, during 1987 when the stock market crashed causing the Index of Leading Economic Indicators to predict a recession or worse, the Purchasing Managers Index was predicting continued strong growth. Of course, the economy did continue to grow until 1990, at which time both indexes foretold the onset of the 1990–91 recession.

Some people are bothered that the Purchasing Managers Index is biased towards manufacturing when in fact the United States is predominantly an information/service economy. I don't believe this is a major problem because the forecasting ability of the index has been so good. This is probably due to the strong interdependence of the manufacturing and service sectors.

Both of these indexes are released around the first of each month. Most of the time they paint the same picture of the economy: growing, flat, or shrinking. If there is an incongruence between the two, I always side with the Purchasing Managers Index. After all, purchasing managers are real people heavily involved in the heart of the economy. Much better to consult these people than a bunch of economists who depend upon secondary data!

How the Business Cycle Can Help with Value Investing

Once you have identified the current stage of the business cycle, what do you do with this information? As you begin a detailed value analysis, the business cycle stage may allow you to identify undervalued industries. As the economy progresses through the business cycle, different industries move in and out of favor with investors. Such changes in investor sentiment may help explain why a particular industry shows up when you are using a PE screen, for example.

More broadly, the market's undervaluation to overvaluation cycle seems to be rooted in the business cycle. As we will see in more detail in the last section of this chapter, the market tends to be undervalued at economic troughs and overvalued at economic peaks. Knowing whether the economy is near a trough or a peak, then, provides a rough indication of the undervaluation or overvaluation of the market as a whole. Near an economic trough, it will be easier generally to find undervalued stocks, while at peaks it will be easier to find overvalued stocks. Thus, you might buy more near troughs and sell more near peaks.

Can the Business Cycle Be Used for Market Timing?

Beyond this relatively passive use, is there more you should do in response to the business cycle? For example, I am often asked whether or not an investor should completely withdraw from the market around economic peaks and then fully invest at economic troughs. This type of market timing is extraordinarily difficult to execute. My own feeling is that you should stay fully invested at all times.

Let the techniques of value investing that we will explore in the following chapters help you tell when to buy and sell. As a consequence, the timing of your investment decisions will be altered "naturally" by the business cycle as its effects are filtered through the value investing.

THE FEDERAL DEFICIT AND MONEY: DO THEY MATTER?

VALUE INVESTING TIPS

▼ In spite of all the articles dealing with the relationship between the budget deficit and the economy, there is little or no evidence that the federal deficit matters.

▼ Money supply growth is important in terms of its effect on inflation.

▼ The relationship between the money supply and the economy is weak and growing weaker over time.

Over the years, Congress and the President have engaged in some vicious battles over balancing the federal budget. Such battles are closely followed by the press and are of great interest to many people in the country. As investors, how important are the results of budget negotiations to the future of the stock market? More broadly, how do decisions of the federal government affect the market? These questions fall into the area of the relationship between fiscal policy and market performance.

Another set of issues revolves around the Federal Reserve and the control of the money supply. How much influence does the Federal Reserve have on the future course of the market? Can the Fed encourage a robust economy without stirring the fearsome inflation monster?

Does Fiscal Policy Matter?

As you watch the numerous titanic struggles between the President and Congress over how to balance the federal budget, you might have wondered whether any of this mattered to you as an investor. The underlying message of these negotiations is that it is important to balance the budget and if it did balance, the country would be economically better off.

The deficit is a major tool of fiscal policy in which the government attempts to arrange the financing of the federal budget in such a way to encourage noninflationary economic growth. The theory is that running a budget deficit by reducing taxes and issuing Treasury bills or bonds stimulates the economy while running a surplus slows down the economy. Even though both taxes and treasuries are paid for by Americans (with the exception of about the 15 percent of treasuries purchased by foreigners), it is theorized that paying higher taxes has a greater dampening effect on current consumption than does the equivalent purchase of treasuries, the funds for which are thought to come more from savings.

The problem is that this theory has not been properly implemented. John Maynard Keynes proposed during the 1930s that the government should run deficits during recessions (and depressions) and run surpluses during expansions. Contrary to theory, the government has run budget deficits for decades, both during recessions and expansions.

Would Eliminating the Deficit Help the Economy?

Will the economy improve if the deficits are eliminated? I have my doubts. The economy has performed quite well over the last 40 years during which time deficits were quite large. The United States currently has the highest standard of living in the world and appears to be improving its international competitiveness. Inflation and interest rates are low as is the unemployment rate. The current widespread anxiety over job security has more to do with technological change than with the budget deficit. It is hard to imagine that the U.S. economy could have done much better during the post-WWII period if deficits had been eliminated.

Actually, a number of studies come to this conclusion: The level of economic activity seems to have little to do with historical U.S. budget deficits. The results of these studies can be viewed either as a refutation of the basic thesis underlying fiscal policy or as an indictment of our government's poor implementation of the concept. Studies across countries come to a similar conclusion: The size of the deficit simply doesn't matter.

The Size of the Government Does Matter

However, the extent to which the government meddles in the private sector does seem to matter. The greater the government involvement, the poorer is economic performance. Thus the focus of the budget talks should really be on reducing the *size* of the government and not on eliminating deficits, per se. However, many, including myself, believe that balancing the budget will lead to a smaller government. So let's balance the budget!

Does the Federal Reserve Influence Inflation and Growth?

The Federal Reserve is the only organization within the United States granted the authority to print money. Federal Reserve Board members are appointed by the President to 14-year terms, so the Fed is largely insulated from short-term political pressures. In managing the nation's money supply, the Fed is trying to create an economic environment characterized by low inflation accompanied by robust economic growth.

The basic equation of exchange for the Fed is as follows:

$$\text{Money supply growth} =$$
$$\text{Inflation} + \text{Real GDP growth}$$

If the money supply grows too fast, then inflation results. This is an investor's worst fear because stocks do not seem to do well in a highly inflationary environment. If the money supply grows too slowly, then economic growth may be stunted. So the Fed tries to strike the right balance. I believe that a money supply growth rate of around 5 percent is desirable. This is consistent with 2 percent inflation and 3 percent real growth.

The problem is that the Fed, as big and important as it is, is a relatively small player in the $7 trillion U.S. economy. The Fed must correctly anticipate the collective behavior of hundreds of banks, thousands of firms and millions of individuals to effectively conduct monetary policy.

Measuring Money Growth Using the Adjusted Monetary Base

Figure 5.7 shows growth rates for the *Adjusted Monetary Base* over which the Fed has the greatest control because it is comprised of currency in circulation and deposits by commercial banks at the Fed. But the problem is that this measure represents only a small fraction of the money actually used by businesses and consumers for day-to-day transactions. Even though the Fed may have a great deal of control over the Adjusted Monetary Base, it is only tangentially related to the "real" money used in the economy.

M1

A broader and more inclusive measure of money is *M1*, which is the sum of the Adjusted Monetary Base, checking account balances and other check-

FIGURE 5.7 Adjusted Monetary Base

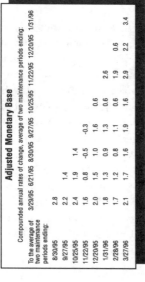

Adjusted Monetary Base

Compounded annual rates of change, average of two maintenance periods ending:

To the average of two maintenance periods ending:	3/29/95	6/21/95	8/30/95	9/27/95	10/25/95	11/22/95	12/20/95	1/31/96
8/30/95	2.8							
9/27/95	2.2	1.4						
10/25/95	2.4	1.9	1.4					
11/22/95	1.6	0.8	-0.5	-0.3				
12/20/95	2.0	1.5	1.0	1.6	0.6			
1/31/96	1.8	1.3	0.9	1.3	0.6	2.6		
2/28/96	1.7	1.2	0.8	1.1	0.6	1.9	0.6	
3/27/96	2.1	1.7	1.6	1.9	1.6	2.9	2.2	3.4

The adjusted monetary base is the sum of reserve accounts of financial institutions of Federal Reserve banks, currency in circulation (currency held by the public and in the vaults of all depository institutions) and an adjustment for reserve requirement ratio changes. The major source of the adjusted monetary base is Federal Reserve credit. Data are computed by this bank. A detailed description of the adjusted monetary base is available from this bank. Recent data are preliminary.

Source: U.S. Financial Data, April 4, 1996, Federal Reserve Bank of St. Louis.

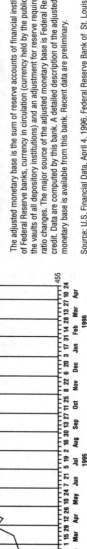

Averages of Daily Figures Seasonally Adjusted

Billions of Dollars

1996	Billions
Jan 17	471.4
31	470.4
Feb 14	470.4
28	471.5
Mar 13	471.7
27	474.9

able deposits. M1 is much closer to what is actually used by market participants. But the problem is that the Fed has much less control over M1 growth. It must count on banks, businesses and individuals to act in a predictable way when making loans, paying bills and spending monthly pay checks. Needless to say, there is a great deal of sloppiness in the Fed's M1 control mechanism. In fact, it is believed that the M1 response window may extend as far as 24 months into the future following a specific Fed action—akin to turning around a supertanker.

M2

An even broader measure of money is *M2,* shown in Figure 5.8, which includes M1 along with savings deposits and other deposits. As you might imagine, the Fed's control over M2 is even sloppier than its control over M1. On the other hand, studies show that growth in M2 is closely related to inflation and GDP growth. In other words, the money over which the Fed has the least control has the greatest impact on the economy.

So Does Money Really Matter?

In terms of inflation, the answer is a definite yes. The Fed can easily ignite inflation by growing the money supply too rapidly. As a stock investor, you should always remain vigilant against this possibility. In terms of economic growth, the answer is not clear. It appears that the Fed has only moderate influence over the future course of the economy. What is more, recent studies have shown that what little influence the Fed once had has weakened in recent years.

World inflationary trends are very encouraging. The inflation rate is dropping around the world both in developed and developing countries. It is premature to claim victory over the inflation dragon, but we seem to be heading in the right direction. Let's hope that the world's central banks continue to show restraint in terms of money supply growth.

VALUING THE MARKETS AS A WHOLE

VALUE INVESTING TIPS

▼ You should begin the market-wide valuation process by identifying the current stage of the business cycle.

▼ You can identify those markets that are undervalued, overvalued or properly valued by calculating the ratio of cash flows to current prices for the various markets and then comparing these ratios to historical averages.

▼ You may want to implement a Tactical Asset Allocation (TAA) strategy based on market-wide valuations using a separate portfolio invested in a variety of mutual funds.

Before you dive into the detailed task of valuing individual stocks, it is useful to determine if the market as a whole is undervalued or overvalued. If the market is undervalued, then it will be easier to find undervalued stocks, and if the market is overvalued, it will be easier to find overvalued stocks. Your pattern of buying and selling may change as the market goes through its undervaluation to overvaluation cycle.

As we discussed in a previous section, the market's undervaluation to overvaluation cycle is influenced by the business cycle. The market tends to be undervalued around an economic trough and overvalued around an economic peak. In conducting the market-wide valuation, you should begin with an analysis of the economy to determine the current stage of the business cycle. This is followed by

FIGURE 5.8 M2

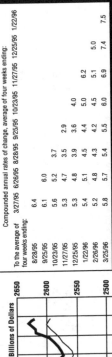

Money Stock M2

Compounded annual rates of change, average of four weeks ending:

To the average of four weeks ending:	3/27/95	6/26/95	8/28/95	9/25/95	10/23/95	11/27/95	12/25/95	1/22/96
8/28/95	6.4							
9/25/95	6.1	6.0						
10/23/95	5.6	5.2	3.7					
11/27/95	5.3	4.7	3.5	2.9				
12/25/95	5.3	4.8	3.9	3.6	4.0			
1/22/96	5.4	5.1	4.5	4.4	5.0	6.2		
2/26/96	5.2	4.8	4.3	4.2	4.5	5.1	5.0	
3/25/96	5.8	5.7	5.4	5.5	6.0	6.9	7.4	7.5

M2 is the sum of M1, savings (including money market deposit accounts), small time deposits and retail money funds. Current data appear in the Federal Reserve Board's H.6 release.

Source: *U.S. Financial Data*, April 4, 1996, Federal Reserve Bank of St. Louis.

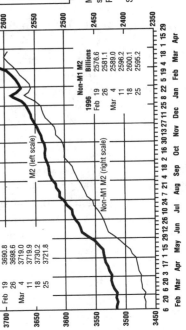

FIGURE 5.9 Economic Summary Form

Economic Summary Form

April 1996
Date

Measure	Time Period	Value	Comment
GDP Real Growth	1995	1.7%	Weak
Index of Leading Indicators	Feb 96	+1.5%	Strong
Purchasing Managers Index	Mar 96	47	Weak
Inflation (CPI)	12 months	2%	Good
Unemployment	Mar 96	5.6%	Good
Money Supply (M2) Growth	12 months	5.8%	Good

a cash-flow-based valuation of various financial markets.

A Snapshot of the Economy

We discussed several important aspects of the economy and the business cycle in the earlier sections of this chapter. Figure 5.9 contains a summary form that provides a snapshot of the economy and helps you determine the current business cycle stage. It includes those series that are the most important for keeping track of the economy.

As an example, the information in Figure 5.9 is for April 1996 and indicates a slow growth economy that is experiencing relatively low unemployment and low inflation. As is frequently the case, it is difficult to determine whether or not the economy is heading into a recession. Nevertheless, the economy is closer to an economic peak than it is to a trough in April 1996, so do not be surprised if later we determine that the stock market is overvalued.

M2 is growing at an acceptable rate, consistent with healthy growth and continued low inflation. You would be concerned if, on the other hand, M2 growth accelerated to 10 percent and beyond. High rates of growth in M2 eventually lead to renewed inflation. The last time this happened was during the late 1970s and early 1980s, a period during which the stock market did very poorly.

Valuing Markets as a Whole

You should identify the fundamental source of value and then relate it to the current price in order to value an entire market. For the stock market, you should focus on both dividends and earnings. You should use interest rates, representing the ratio of cash flow (i.e., interest payments) to the current price, for valuing other markets. Thus for each market, you will form the ratio of income (the fundamental source of value) to the current price.

The appropriate ratio will be compared to its historical average to determine if a particular market is undervalued or overvalued. The idea behind this technique is that the basic relationship between cash flow and value changes little over time. That is, investors today collectively demand the same return for the same level of risk as they did 20 or 50 or even 100 years ago. The evidence presented earlier in Figure 2.2 in which real market returns were virtually identical during the three subperiods of 1802–1870, 1871–1925 and 1926–1992 provides support for this contention.

If the current value of the ratio deviates from its historical average, then the market is considered to be undervalued or overvalued. The greater is this difference, the greater is the undervaluation or overvaluation.

Are the Markets Properly Valued?

Figure 5.10 presents April 1996 market-wide valuations for several markets. The starting point is the current inflation rate that allows you to determine if T-bills are properly valued. Historically the T-bill rate has averaged 1 percent over the inflation

FIGURE 5.10   Market Summary Form

Market Summary Form

April 1996
_____
Date

Measure	Current Value	Historical Average	Comment
Inflation	2%	3%	Good
90-day T-Bill	5%	3%	Undervalued
Long-term T-Bond	6.8%	6%	Undervalued
AAA Bond Premium	.6%	.6%	Property Valued
BAA Bond Premium	1.2%	1.2%	Property Valued
Dividend Yield	2.5%	3%	Overvalued
PE Ratio	16	14	Overvalued

rate. The current real T-bill return of 5 percent indicates that T-bills are undervalued relative to the current inflation rate.

Bond Market Valuations

The three bond markets are valued based on the interest rate premium relative to the next best alternative investment. For the long-term T-bond, the 1.8 percent extra return earned above the T-bill rate exceeds the historical average of 1 percent. Thus T-bonds seem to be undervalued relative to T-bills. A different conclusion is reached for both the AAA corporate bond and the BAA corporate bond: Each risk premium above the T-bond rate is equal to its respective historical average. Consequently T-bonds seem to offer the best investment opportunity among bonds.

Valuing the Stock Market

However, the stock market tells a different story. Both the dividend yield as well as the PE ratio indicates some degree of overvaluation. A *low* yield indicates overvaluation while a *high* PE also indicates overvaluation. This result is consistent with the earlier conclusion that the economy is closer to a cyclical peak than to a trough.

A Constantly Changing Valuation Mosaic

In summary, the April 1996 T-bill and T-bond markets seem to be undervalued while the stock market seems to be a bit overvalued and the other bond markets are properly valued. This is the market-wide valuation picture with which you begin your value analysis. This picture changes constantly, so it is necessary to redo the economic snapshot along with the market-wide valuations several times a year. Both of these summaries provide the economic and market contexts in which you are analyzing individual stocks.

Tactical Asset Allocation

Tactical Asset Allocation (TAA) is a market timing technique that tries to exploit the undervaluation and overvaluation of various markets. The idea behind TAA is quite simple: Increase your investment in undervalued markets while decreasing your investment in overvalued markets. The problem you encounter is how to implement TAA without affecting your basic stock selection strategy. In general, you do not want to disturb your basic strategy, so you will have to implement TAA as a separate portfolio.

Consequently, you will have to set up a second portfolio comprised of a money market mutual fund, bond mutual fund and a stock mutual fund to implement a TAA strategy. You will then reallocate among these three markets as their relative valuations change. For example, in April 1996 you would increase your T-bill and T-bond allocations while decreasing your stock allocation. If you pursue such a strategy, you can expect a three-year to five-year allocation cycle, again strongly influenced by the underlying business cycle.

Again, you should not use your individual stock portfolio to implement the TAA strategy. It is too difficult to run both of these strategies on the same portfolio because too many conflicts will arise and transactions costs will probably overwhelm any possible gain.

CHAPTER 6

▼ ▼ ▼

Untangling Financial Statements

VALUE INVESTOR'S CHECKLIST

✓ Financial statements represent the starting point for all quantitative stock analysis.

✓ Revenues, earnings, cash flow and dividends are very important for stock valuation.

✓ The balance sheet can play an important role in value investing if you are a conservative investor or if the company is experiencing financial distress.

✓ Financial ratio analysis helps you decide whether or not to proceed with a detailed value analysis of the stock.

✓ If the firms' accountants and managers strongly disagree over the story to be told, you can often find the controversy reported in the financial footnotes.

FLOWS: REVENUES, EARNINGS, CASH FLOW AND DIVIDENDS

VALUE INVESTING TIPS

▼ As a potential or current shareholder, you are most interested in the money flows being produced by the company.

▼ The value of a stock is a direct function of these money flows as they determine the amount and timing of the cash returned to you.

▼ Money flows are important even for stocks not presently paying dividends because at some future time you expect to receive cash back for your investment.

At a very basic level, the success of a stock is a direct consequence of the money flows generated by the underlying company. A company that is generating a great deal of money per dollar invested is relatively more successful than the company that is producing a smaller amount of money per dollar invested.

The money flows of the company begin with revenues. Out of revenues are paid operating and financial expenses. The amount left over is the earnings (or profits or net income) of the company. Certain noncash expenses are deducted in calculating earnings (most notably depreciation and depletion), so some analysts feel that a better measure of the company's "earning power" can be obtained by adding back these noncash expenses to obtain what is called cash flow. The final flow, and to the stock investor the most important, is dividends that are paid out of earnings.

Where Do You Obtain Financial Information?

Before we dive into the details of the income statement, a few words about where you can obtain financial information about a company. For most investors, it is preferable to get this information from an investment service such as *Value Line Investment Survey* or *S&P Stock Reports*. The reason is that such services provide not only the raw data but also a wealth of company analysis. Much of what the company's annual report contains, on the other hand, is of little help to potential investors, except for the financial statements and footnotes.

If you use a computer, as I do, you can gather the needed information from databases such as the *American Association of Individual Investors Stock Investor, Market Base, Value Line's Value Screen* or from various online services. Generally, each service also provides industry-wide as well as market-wide summary statistics.

Recognizing Revenues

The headwaters of the money flow river are the revenues generated by selling the company's goods and services. Obviously, without sales the company has no chance of generating anything downstream such as earnings or dividends. Thus it is reasonable to use revenues as a gauge of value.

Measuring revenues is not as straightforward as it might seem. The primary issue is to determine the point in time at which a sales contract can be counted as revenue. In a typical business situation, the customer places an order for the product or service, the company prepares and delivers the product or service, the company sends a bill, and finally the customer pays the bill. Completing all these steps may take weeks, months or even years.

When should the company recognize the revenues associated with this sale? U.S. accounting standards are quite conservative on this issue and allow for revenue recognition only when the effort to produce and deliver the product or service is largely complete, ownership has passed to the buyer, and there is a strong probability that the bill will be paid by the buyer.

Latitude in Reporting Revenues

But even with a carefully specified set of rules, there is considerable latitude in reporting revenues. While inappropriate revenue recognition is a potential problem with any company, smaller growing companies are more likely to stretch this rule to the limit. A couple of recent examples might be enlightening.

In the early days of the Home Shopping Network (HSN), fur coats and computers were being offered. The sales of these products were strong and were recorded as revenues. But the customer return rate on both these products was much higher than expected, so HSN had to restate revenues, much to the consternation of shareholders.

In another case, MiniScribe, a maker of hard disk drives for personal computers, recorded as revenues shipments to their own warehouses. The units did not sell, so again revenues had to be restated. In this case, however, the premature recognition of revenue was a small part of a massive fraud perpetrated by management. Eventually MiniScribe filed for bankruptcy, and several senior managers faced criminal charges.

These two examples represent extreme cases of premature revenue recognition to the detriment of shareholders. If you suspect that the company you are analyzing might be recognizing revenues inappropriately, you can check the footnotes to the income statement. They will sometimes provide a hint of a problem. In addition, potential problems are sometimes reported in the press or can be detected by comparing the company to a close competitor.

Rules for Recording Expenses

Much like revenues, there is a wide range of possible expense reporting rules. It might be plausible to record a *direct* production expense when the item is purchased, when the supplier is actually paid, when the item is placed in or taken out of inventory, when it is used for manufacturing the product, when the final product is sold or when the final customer pays for the product. For *indirect* expenses, on the other hand, little linkage exists between the production and sales process, so when to record such expenses is an open question. Accountants follow two basic rules in reporting expenses.

The Matching Principle

The first rule is that *direct* production expenses are recorded at the same time the corresponding revenue is realized. This approach makes it much clearer to you whether or not the company is profitable at the most basic level. This concept is known as the *Matching Principle*.

An important Matching Principle issue is how to keep track of inventory. Should the company "sell" the oldest item in the inventory (known as FIFO, or first in, first out), or should it "sell" the newest item (known as LIFO, or last in, first out)? During periods of low inflation, such as is currently the case, the choice of inventory accounting has little effect. But as inflation picks up, companies move to LIFO accounting so that earnings are not overstated. In the high inflation of the late 1970s and early 1980s, the LIFO or FIFO question was a major accounting issue.

Overhead Expenses

The second expense reporting approach is to record *indirect* or *overhead* expenses at the time they are incurred. This disconnection between expenses and revenue causes difficulties in conducting financial analysis, but there seems to be no other way to record these expenses.

A significant part of the overhead expense is depreciation, which in a way is an expense and in a way is not. The actual outflow for a piece of equipment or a building occurs when it is initially purchased. But it does not make sense to record this entire expenditure at that time because the equipment will be "used up" over a long period of time. Therefore, the cost is allocated over an extended period of time or in accounting vernacular, *depreciated*. In this respect, depreciation is an accounting creation and not a true cash expense.

Reported Earnings

Earnings, being a residual of revenues over expenses, can be devilishly difficult to estimate. A small change in either revenues or expenses can lead to substantial changes in earnings. This is demonstrated by the sensitivity analysis in the two right columns in Figure 6.1 in which ABC Cruise Lines' (a fictitious company) revenues are increased by 10 percent then decreased by 10 percent. The resulting change in earnings is +25 percent and –25 percent, respectively.

Now, you might be thinking that if revenues change, so should expenses and thus earnings should be little affected. This is true in the long run, but over shorter periods, revenue surprises are generally not offset by expense changes and so indeed earnings are more volatile than are revenues. This is why an earnings surprise is generally greater than is the corresponding revenue surprise.

Many analysts believe that earnings per share (EPS) is the most important flow for the company. After all it is the best estimate of the company's profitability and to a large extent determines whether the company will survive and thrive or decline and fail. As you will see later in this chapter, the ratio of EPS to shareholder equity, referred to as return on equity (ROE), is the best

FIGURE 6.1   ABC Cruise Lines Financial Flows

	Actuals (In $ Millions)	Sensitivity Analysis			
		Revenues up 10%	(% Change)	Revenues down 10%	(% Change)
Revenues	$1,171	$1,288	+10%	$1,054	–10%
Operating	729	802		656	
General and Administrative	224	224		224	
Gross Profit	218	262		174	
Interest Payments	43	43		43	
Taxes Paid	33	41		25	
Earnings	142	178	+25%	106	–25%
Shares Outstanding	63.40	63.40		63.40	
Per Share Figures:					
Earnings	2.24	2.81	+25%	1.67	–25%
Depreciation	1.23	1.23		1.23	
Cash Flow	3.47	4.04	+16%	2.90	–16%
Capital Expenditures	2.73	2.73		2.73	
Net Free Cash Flow	0.74	1.31	+76%	0.17	–76%
Dividends	0.44	0.44		0.44	

Note: Sensitivity analysis assumes G&A and interest payments are fixed and all other expenses are variable.

accounting indicator of the company's investment performance. It captures the two most important events for shareholders: investing money in the company and then earning a return.

Reducing the Distorting Effects of Depreciation by Using Cash Flow

Some analysts believe that *cash flow per share*, the sum of EPS and noncash expenses, primarily depreciation, provides a less distorted picture of the company's earning power. Cash flow per share includes the tax-reducing effects of depreciation while excluding noncash depreciation itself. The cash flow per share for ABC is shown in the lower part of Figure 6.1. Note that it is less sensitive to changes in revenue than is EPS.

Net Free Cash Flow

Some argue that cash flow overstates the earning power of the company because it does not account for the company's capital expenditures. While depreciation is a somewhat arbitrary noncash expense, it is intended to measure the real cost of the normal wear and tear on equipment, buildings and other physical assets. To exclude such expenses entirely, as does cash flow, seems to be going too far.

Net free cash flow per share is calculated by subtracting capital expenditures per share from the previously calculated cash flow per share and is shown for ABC at the bottom of Figure 6.1. Some analysts argue that this is the best measure of the company's earning power because it includes both the tax sheltering effect of depreciation along with a superior estimate of asset wear and tear in the form of actual capital expenditures. You can see in Figure 6.1 that net free cash flow is very sensitive to revenue changes.

Dividends

The final flow and the bottom line for an investor is dividends. Unlike the previous flows of revenues, earnings and cash flow, no accounting controversies surround the dividend number reported by the company. The dividend is the amount of money paid to shareholders, period.

The vast majority of companies that actually pay dividends (most U.S. companies do *not* pay dividends) follow a stable dividend policy. This means that dividends are raised only when the new dividend payment can be maintained into the foreseeable future and the company is loathe to ever reduce dividends.

In a sense, then, the company is trying to signal its long-term earnings power by the size of its dividend payments. Because company insiders have access to information that is not available to the average investor, management's decision to raise and, heaven forbid, lower dividends should convey new information to the market. Studies indeed confirm this, as stock prices tend to increase with an announced dividend increase and fall with an announced decrease in dividends.

Retaining Only What Can Be Profitably Invested

Currently the average U.S. company traded on the NYSE is paying out 35 percent of earnings in the form of dividends. Some argue that this is too low, that more earnings should be paid out as dividends. This is based on the premise that a company should retain only those earnings for which it can earn a return higher than can shareholders elsewhere (about 10 percent to 12 percent). If the company does not have such opportunities, earnings should be returned to shareholders in the form of dividends, giving the shareholders an opportunity to invest in another company.

A couple of barriers stand in the way of this optimal view of management behavior. First, management is generally reluctant to give money back that is already in the firm. "We can find *something* to do with this money" might summarize their thought process. It is only human nature to hoard like this, so shareholders need to remain ever vigilant against the unreasonable accumulation of cash within the company. The rash of takeovers over the last 15 years and the resulting emphasis by management on maximizing shareholder value have to some extent curbed this abuse.

The tax law is the second thing standing in the way of the proper dividend distribution. Dividends are taxed immediately while capital gains are taxed only when the stock is sold. Thus there is a built-in bias toward retaining rather than paying out dividends. In recent years, some companies have addressed this problem by repurchasing shares rather than paying dividends.

ASSETS, LIABILITIES AND SHAREHOLDER EQUITY

VALUE INVESTING TIPS

▼ The balance sheet plays a much less important role in value investing than does the income statement.

▼ If you are a conservative investor, you will spend more time examining the financing part of the balance sheet, particularly the company's debt structure.

▼ Shareholder equity is of interest to you because it represents the accumulation of all moneys invested in the company by shareholders.

The balance sheet for a company represents a snapshot of the company's financial situation, portraying the existing relationship among assets, liabilities and shareholder equity. For you, it provides an indication of the company's state of health and some information on the company's ability to continue operating in the future. However, the information on the balance sheet is most helpful when it is placed in the context of the cash flows being produced by the company. Thus the assets, liabilities and shareholder equity are viewed as a means to an end and not an end in themselves.

More Important for the Conservative Investor

The balance sheet will play a more prominent role if you are a conservative investor. You might analyze the debt structure of the company as a way to gauge the chance of financial distress or, at the extreme, bankruptcy. If the company is currently experiencing some sort of financial distress, such as a delay in making interest payments, the balance sheet will be of greater interest irrespective of how conservative you are because continued financial distress or possible bankruptcy will have an important effect on your valuation of the company.

What the Company Owns: Assets

The company's assets are reported on the left-hand side of the balance sheet and are broken down into two broad categories: current and fixed. *Current assets* consist of cash as well as financial and nonfinancial assets, which have a maturity of one year or less. Figure 6.2 shows that ABC Cruise Lines reports four current asset categories: cash, short-term securities, *accounts receivable* (money owed to ABC by others) and inventory.

Why Does a Company Hold Cash?

You can easily understand why ABC would purchase ships, dishes, tables and the like because no customer would consider cruising without these essential assets. But why does the company hold cash since it provides no return? The answer is that a certain level of cash is needed to facilitate day-to-day transactions (Almost no supplier will take a cruise ship as payment for services rendered!). However, much like limiting the amount of cash you carry in your billfold, the company should limit the amount of cash held.

For similar reasons, the company should limit investment in short-term securities. The return on such securities is much lower (for a typical company, about 6 percent to 7 percent lower) than what the company can earn on other business opportunities. The only reasons for holding such securities are as a temporary parking place for cash or as a buffer against unforeseen misfortunes. As we saw in the previous section, management is prone to keep too much money inside the company rather

FIGURE 6.2 ABC Cruise Lines Balance Sheet (in $ Millions)

Assets

Cash & Equivalent	$ 24	
Short-term Securities	9	
Accounts Receivable	61	
Inventory	24	
Total Current Assets		$ 118
Net Property, Plan, Equipment	1,382	
Other Long-term Assets	365	
Total Long-term Assets		$1,747
Total Assets		**$1,865**

Liabilities and Shareholder Equity

Accounts Receivable	$ 63	
Bank Loans	61	
Customer Deposits	148	
Total Current Liabilities		$ 272
Long-term Debt	$748	
Shareholder Equity:		
Paid-in Capital	301	
Retained Earnings	547	
Treasury Stock	(3)	
Other Adjustments	–	
Total Capital		$1,593
Total Liabilities & Equity		**$1,865**

than pay it out to shareholders. If this is indeed the case, it will show up as too much invested in short-term securities.

Accounts Receivable and Inventory

The amounts invested in accounts receivable and inventory are largely determined by the competitive nature of the industry. Since ABC is a service company as compared to a manufacturing company, inventories are relatively small.

In recent years, the new way that inventories are managed has played a key role in the restructuring of the economy. With the advent of advanced computer technology and just-in-time inventory methods, the inventory structure of the U.S. economy has changed dramatically. But even with these changes, a buildup of inventory can foreshadow a sales slowdown at the company level or even at the economy level.

Fixed Assets

Long-term or *fixed assets* are the physical items that are essential to the operations of the company. For ABC, it is essential that they own (or lease) ships and all the furniture and other items necessary to create a quality cruise experience for their customers. But as important as these assets are, the company should be ever vigilant to avoid investing too much in fixed assets. Again, they are a means and not an end in themselves. ABC's balance sheet in Figure 6.2 shows that 96 percent of assets are long-term. This indicates that fixed assets play a predominate role relative to current assets.

What the Company Owes: Liabilities

The top portion of the right side of the balance sheet lists the current and long-term liabilities or simply the company's debt. Unlike the small role played by current assets, *current liabilities* or debt obligations due within a year are relatively more important for ABC, making up 26 percent of total liabilities and 15 percent of total financing. Current liabilities are comprised primarily of *accounts receivable* (money ABC owes to others), short-term money market instruments such as commercial paper (not used by ABC) and bank loans.

Note the small role played by bank loans, representing only 3 percent of total financing. This is typical of U.S. companies as the stock, bond and other "public" markets are used to meet most external funding needs. This is quite different in many other countries where banks play a much more important financing role.

Is Using Debt Bad?

Before moving onto the last component of the balance sheet, shareholder equity, I would like to address the popular misconception that debt is bad. The ultimate conclusion of this line of thinking is that the best company is the one with little or no debt. An ultraconservative investor might hew to this line, but for most investors, debt financing should not present a problem. In fact, debt financing (e.g., bank loans, commercial paper or bonds) has a distinct advantage in that interest payments are tax deductible while stock dividends are not.

Debt should be viewed as one of many financing sources available to the firm. Much like ABC offers a variety of cruise packages to appeal to a wide range of potential customers, management offers a variety of ways to invest in the company. This financing variety reduces the average cost of financing to ABC as well as allowing it to raise the necessary funds.

Money market securities, such as commercial paper and banker's acceptances, appeal to those investors with a high need for liquidity and predictability. Bonds appeal to those investors with a high need for long-term, predictable income. Stocks appeal to those investors willing to take on considerable business risk in hopes of high average returns.

Beyond these standard financing instruments (referred to as *bulge bracket* securities because the vast majority of investors prefer them), companies have a number of other types of securities they can offer to attract investors. These include preferred stock, convertible bonds, warrants and many other types, limited only by the imagination of investment bankers.

Therefore, debt is simply one choice among a veritable panoply of financing vehicles. In the next section, we will discuss how you can determine if the company has gone too far in its use of debt.

What Stock Investors Own: Shareholder Equity

The last element on the balance sheet and probably the most important is shareholder equity (or book value or net worth). It is the last entry on the lower right hand side of the balance sheet in Figure 6.2. *Shareholder equity* is the accumulation over time of all types of shareholder investments in the company, net of cash outflows such as the repurchase of shares. The four major components of shareholder equity are paid-in-capital, retained earnings, treasury stock and other adjustments.

Paid-In Capital

Paid-in capital is the amount received by the company for the initial public sale of stock. Often this amount is arbitrarily split into two parts by means of the company setting a *par value* (arbitrary stock value for legal purposes). Most companies issue shares infrequently, so paid-in capital generally remains unchanged from year to year. ABC issued 8 million new shares during 1993, raising about $200 million in new equity capital. This was the only new share issue by ABC over the past ten years (this information can be obtained from the annual report).

Retained Earnings

Figure 6.2 reports that ABC's retained earnings represent about 65 percent of shareholder equity. Management finds it much easier to retain earnings, which are already in the company, than issue new shares or bonds or request a new loan from a bank. For investors, this can be both good and bad. If the company has good business investment opportunities, then investors are quite happy that management has easy access to earnings. But if attractive opportunities don't exist, then investors are not pleased when management retains earnings simply because they are there for the keeping. We have discussed this cash hoarding problem already.

Buying Back Shares

Management can disgorge excess cash by buying back shares, which shows up as *treasury stock* and leads to a reduction in shareholder equity. In recent years, more and more firms have repurchased shares. Why does a company repurchase shares rather than use the excess cash to increase dividends? One reason is that the company may be following a stable dividend policy (the most popular dividend strategy among companies) and is reluctant to increase dividends for fear that the higher rate cannot be maintained. Repurchasing shares disgorges excess cash and avoids this dilemma.

Another problem with increasing dividends is that dividends paid represent a current tax event for each and every shareholder. A share repurchase, on the other hand, represents a tax event only for those shareholders who actually sell their shares to the company. Both the company and their shareholders find this voluntary taxation feature attractive.

Share Repurchase Distorts the Value of Shareholder Equity

While there are several advantages to the shareholder of share repurchase, there is a significant analytic disadvantage. Usually the shares are repurchased at a price that is higher than the current *book value per share* (shareholder equity divided by the number of shares outstanding). In fact, as a shareholder you hope that this is the case because it implies the company has successfully invested shareholder money to produce greater value (recently the median price to book ratio for the S&P 500 was 2.5).

But the problem is that each share repurchased wipes out a larger number of "book shares." This means that if ABC, for example, repurchased 68 percent (current price to book ratio of 1.47) of its shares, all the accounting shareholder equity would be wiped out! This leads to the obviously confusing situation in which accounting shareholder value is zero while the market value of ABC would be over $600 million (the precise amount is difficult to estimate because the market typically responds positively to a share repurchase by bidding up the price of the remaining shares).

The source of this problem is that standard accounting practices do not allow for adjusting shareholder equity to reflect the current market value. Consequently, a company that aggressively repurchases shares produces a downward bias in its shareholder equity account. This distorts any calculation involving shareholder equity, such as the return on equity or the price-to-book ratio.

Other Adjustments

The last component of shareholder equity is "other adjustments." These represent accounting and other changes that do not flow through the income statement. The most common of these is the *currency translation adjustment,* which reflects gains and losses elsewhere in the balance sheet resulting from foreign currency fluctuations. Most often, other adjustments are of little consequence to stock investors.

MAKING FINANCIAL STATEMENTS USEFUL: RATIO ANALYSIS

VALUE INVESTING TIPS

▼ Ratio analysis is a way for you to standardize financial statements so that you can compare them to another company, the industry and the market as a whole.

▼ A standard ratio analysis focuses on the company's growth potential, profitability, valuation and financial structure.

▼ A ratio analysis is an efficient way for you to determine if the company is worth further analysis.

Now that we have looked at each component of the income statement and balance sheet, how do you go about analyzing them? For example, how do you determine if the company has taken on the right amount of debt? How do you measure the profitability of the company's business investments? How can you tell if management is hoarding cash? The answer to these and other questions will dictate whether or not you invest in a particular stock.

Standardizing Financial Statements

Before you can answer these questions, the financial statements have to be standardized by removing the size of the company. This is essential because no two companies are the same size, and indeed the same company varies in size from year to year. So to say that a company's revenues are $1.2 billion with earnings of $154 million tells you little other than that the company is reasonably large and

FIGURE 6.3 Potential Growth Analysis for ABC

Ratio	ABC	XYZ	Recreational Activities Industry	NYSE
5-Year Earnings Growth	22.6%	12.8%	7.8%	6.0%
5-Year Dividend Growth	NA	5.6	7.9	3.2

Source for Industry and NYSE medians is *AAII Stock Investor,* January 31, 1996, edition.

is earning a positive profit (not a bad start, however!).

Ratio Benchmarks

To get a clearer picture, we will calculate ratios for ABC in four general areas: growth potential, profitability, valuation and financial structure. Each ratio will be compared to three benchmarks: XYZ Corporation (a fictitious, similar sized operator of cruise ships), the recreational activities industry (the real industry, which includes 23 companies) and the NYSE (ABC is traded on the NYSE). For comparison purposes, we will use the median (50 percent of companies above and 50 percent below this value) rather than the average because the average is unduly influenced by extreme values, a common problem when using financial data. You can take the further step of comparing the ratios to the upper and lower quartile values (25 percent above and 25 percent below, respectively) for each benchmark.

Growth Potential

The most important determinant of stock value is its future growth potential. Again, as we discussed

FIGURE 6.4   Profitability Analysis for ABC

Ratio	ABC	XYZ	Recreational Activities Industry	NYSE
Net Profit Margin (earnings/ revenues)	13.1%	22.6%	5.8%	5.8%
Return on Equity (ROE) (earnings/ shareholder equity)	16.0	19.2	9.5	12.0

Source for Industry and NYSE medians is *AAII Stock Investor,* January 31, 1996, edition.

in Chapter 4, the focus on growth is only in the context of value and not the other way around. We are looking for value stocks and not growth stocks. So to start the ratio analysis, we will focus on ABC's growth potential.

Figure 6.3 shows ABC's five-year earnings and dividend growth rates. Why five years? Many argue that this is long enough to capture the typical business cycle, which is on average five years in length, while it is not so long as to mask fundamental changes in the company and the industry.

The earnings growth for ABC has been very strong regardless of whether the benchmark is XYZ, the industry or the NYSE. The five-year dividend growth rate is not available as ABC began paying dividends in 1993. Overall I would conclude that ABC's growth potential looks very good. We will discuss additional techniques for measuring growth potential in the next two chapters.

Profitability

Figure 6.4 presents two measures of profitability. The first is the *net profit margin*, which measures the amount that winds up on the bottom line per dollar of revenue. For ABC, this ratio is 13.1, which means that for every dollar of revenue, 13.1 cents is left after covering all business and financial expenses. This is not as strong as XYZ's net profit margin but exceeds the industry average. This ratio is very much driven by the unique competitive environment facing the company. Therefore, the comparison to XYZ is probably more relevant (the recreational services industry includes such disparate companies as Golf Enterprises and Walt Disney) because the two companies face virtually the same competitive environment. For this same reason, the NYSE median is probably the least relevant comparison.

The next measure of profitability is *return on equity* (ROE). ROE is the ratio of earnings to shareholder equity and is the best accounting measure of ABC's success in investing shareholder capital. ABC's ROE is very strong relative to each benchmark, except for XYZ's. Unlike the net profit margin, it does make sense to compare the ROE to each of the three benchmarks. Looking at both profitability measures together, I would conclude that ABC is a solidly profitable company, although not as profitable as is XYZ.

Upward Bias in ROE

ROE is susceptible to the aforementioned downward bias in shareholder equity resulting from the aggressive repurchase of stock. A downward bias in shareholder equity leads to an upward bias in ROE. The treasury stock component in ABC's balance sheet (Figure 6.2) is small, indicating that ABC has not repurchased many shares, so ROE is probably not biased upward.

However, this bias can be a significant problem and may in fact render ROE meaningless. Some analysts have gone so far as to say that there has been so much share repurchase that ROE is a worthless measure. I am not ready to completely

FIGURE 6.5 Valuation Analysis for ABC

Ratio	ABC	XYZ	Recreational Activities Industry	NYSE
Price to Earnings (PE)	9.4	17.0	17.1	16.5
Price to Book (PB)	1.5	3.3	1.8	1.9
Dividend Yield (DPS/ price)	2.3%	1.3%	0.0%	1.1%

Source for Industry and NYSE medians is *AAII Stock Investor,* January 31, 1996, edition.

give up on ROE, but it definitely has its limitations as a measure of profitability.

Valuation

The ratios in Figure 6.5 represent a first signal of whether ABC is undervalued or overvalued. The three ratios are the PE ratio, the *price to book* (PB, which is price per share/book value per share) and the dividend yield. The first two ratios are lower than each of the three benchmarks, while the dividend yield is higher than each of the three benchmarks. All three ratios are therefore flashing a preliminary indication of undervaluation.

This conclusion is further strengthened by the earlier observation that ABC is a profitable and rapidly growing company. I therefore conclude that ABC is a strong candidate for further value analysis.

Financial Structure

The set of ratios in Figure 6.6 deal with the financial or debt structure of ABC. As we discussed

FIGURE 6.6 Financial Structure Analysis for ABC

Ratio	ABC	XYZ	Recreational Activities Industry	NYSE
Current (Current Assets/ Current Liab.)	0.4	0.4	1.0	1.6
LT Debt to Capital (capital is sum of LT debt, preferred stock, share-holder eq.)	49.0%	32.9%	33.0%	33.0%

Source for Industry and NYSE medians is *AAII Stock Investor,* January 31, 1996, edition.

in the previous section, these ratios will be important if you are a very conservative investor or if the firm is experiencing financial distress. The former varies from investor to investor while the latter does not seem to be the case for ABC.

The *current ratio* (current assets/current liabilities) is equal to or lower than each of the three benchmarks. Normally this would be a source of concern because it is an indication of a weak ability to meet short-term bills. But this ratio, like the net profit margin, is strongly influenced by the company's competitive environment. The fact that both ABC and XYZ have the same current ratio is reassuring.

The long-term *debt-to-capital ratio* (LT debt/total capital) at 49 percent for ABC is on the high side, exceeding all three benchmarks. This indicates that there is not much of a cushion against hard times. This seems to be the weakest aspect of ABC and should be carefully explored as part of the upcoming value analysis. A more conservative investor than myself might very well conclude that ABC's debt structure is too risky and decide to eliminate it from further consideration at this point. However, being more aggressive, I would recommend further analysis with a special focus on ABC's debt structure.

LIES, DAMN LIES AND FINANCIAL STATEMENTS

Investors often ask me whether they can trust financial statements such as a company's income statement and balance sheet. The answer is that financial statements are unreliable except when compared to the alternative! That is, they are imperfect, but most are better than having nothing at all. U.S. accounting standards are the strictest in the world, yet they still allow a great deal of reporting latitude. So management has the freedom to paint a rosier picture than really exists in the company.

Can you do anything to check the accuracy of financial statements? Most often it is probably not worth your time to do additional checking. If the financials are misleading, then you can consider that as one of the risks of investing.

However, if you cannot be this sanguine about management misleading you, you can watch for several warning signs:

- If the company regularly changes its auditor, it indicates that a severe conflict exists between management and the auditors about how the financial situation of the firm is being portrayed.
- Another warning sign is an issuance of a qualified opinion by the auditor in the annual report. Reading the auditor's statement will reveal reporting problems encountered by the auditor.
- If you have the time and patience, reading the footnotes to the financials sometimes reveals a wealth of information. It is in the footnotes

that management and the auditor bury their minor and sometimes major differences. Reading them might allow you to gain a more accurate picture of a company's financial situation.

Will taking such precautions eliminate the risk of management pulling a fast one on you? The answer is no. The accounting profession agrees that a management team bent on deceiving investors can get around the best-conceived financial controls and the most tenacious auditor. Only time will uncover such misdeeds.

In one of the more notorious cases in recent years, MiniScribe, a PC hard disk manufacturer headquartered in Colorado, issued fraudulent financial statements for three years before being found out. They went so far as to ship bricks and record them as disk drives! My accounting colleagues tell me that earlier detection would have been extremely difficult due to the widespread nature of the conspiracy within the company.

The good news is that such extreme cases of fraud are rare due to stringent U.S. accounting standards. The bad news is that when it does occur, even the auditors have a difficult time uncovering it.

CHAPTER 7

▼ ▼ ▼

Estimating Value

VALUE INVESTOR'S CHECKLIST

✓ The valuation of stocks based on revenues, earnings, cash flow or dividends is at the heart of value investing.

✓ The signal you will look for is whether or not the stock falls outside the estimated value range.

✓ You are trying to avoid paying for hype and want to value the stock strictly on fundamentals.

✓ Valuation is reasonably straightforward for large, stable companies with a long dividend history.

✓ At the extreme, it becomes impossible to assign a value to a new stock in a new industry with no comparison benchmarks.

✓ For larger, more stable companies you can estimate a value range using the constant growth dividend valuation model.

✓ You can apply the earnings valuation model to a wide range of stocks, both dividend paying and zero dividend stocks.

✓ Valuation models based on cash flow, revenues and book value use an appropriate value multiple for estimating a value range.

VALUATION CONCEPTS

VALUE INVESTING TIPS

▼ Valuation is the process of determining the maximum price you are willing to pay for a stock.

▼ In the simplest case where the stock pays a constant dividend for the foreseeable future, the value of the stock is the price that produces an annual cash flow rate of return equal to the current interest rate on comparable investments.

▼ Stock dividends usually grow over time, so the resulting extra value has to be captured by the valuation model.

▼ Valuation becomes more obtuse when the company pays minimal or zero dividends or if the company's financial history is sparse.

The value of a stock is the maximum price you are willing to pay for the stock. Being a hard-nosed investor, you will base this value on the fundamentals of the company, primarily the present and future monetary flows generated by the company. The present flows are easy to value, but the future ones are more difficult because they involve both the level of interest rates and expected growth.

As you move from large, stable companies to smaller, rapidly growing concerns, you will have more difficulty assigning the correct value to the stock. In doing so, you will progress from valuing dividends to valuing earnings (the most popular approach) to valuing cash flows to valuing almost anything for which there is information (i.e., revenues, assets, book value or even the management team).

The Simplest Valuation Case

Imagine that you want to buy a stock that is paying an annual dividend of $1 per share, and as far as you can tell, this dividend will persist for the foreseeable future. Some utilities come very close to this situation as do many nonconvertible and noncallable long-term government and corporate bonds. What is the value of this stock, or in other words, what is the maximum price you are willing to pay for the stock?

The answer to this question depends, to some extent, on the other investment opportunities available to you. Let's say that the annual interest rate is 10 percent on comparable investments. *Comparable* means that the alternative investments are of the same level of default risk and have roughly the same maturity. In this transparent example, $10 is the value of the stock because by paying this price and receiving a DPS (dividend per share) of $1 per year, your cash flow return is 10 percent, exactly equal to the interest rate. You are therefore indifferent about investing in this particular stock or in a comparable investment.

More generally, the value (V) of a stock paying a constant DPS and being compared to an investment bearing an interest rate (R), is given by the equation

$$V = DPS/R$$

For calculation purposes, the interest rate (R) is represented in fractional form rather than as a percent (i.e., as 0.10 rather than 10 percent). Thus the calculation for the above example is:

$$V = \$1/0.10 = \$10$$

The Source of Value and the Value Multiple

A couple things are worth noting about this valuation equation. First, the value of the stock is based on a DPS of $1 and a value multiple of 10. That is, you are willing to pay 10 times DPS for this stock. The dividend is the *source* of value, and 10 is the *value multiple*. This basic framework will be used for each valuation method: a source of value (DPS, EPS, etc.) combined with a value multiple.

Second, the value multiple in this case depends strictly on the interest rate, R. If R increases to, say, 12 percent, the value multiple will decrease to 8.33 (i.e., $1/0.12 = 8.33$). If R decreases to, say, 8 percent, the value multiple will increase to 12.50 (i.e., $1/0.08 = 12.50$). Not only is R the only information needed for calculating the value multiple, but also the relationship is a negative one: As R increases, value decreases and vice versa. You may be familiar with this relationship from investing in bonds.

Introducing Growth

The previous example is useful for valuing only a limited number of no-growth stocks. In general, however, you expect DPS to grow over time as the company grows. Thus the value of the stock will depend not only on the interest rate, R, but also the dividend growth rate, G. The dividend growth valuation equation will be presented in the next section.

Introducing growth into the valuation equation changes the calculation considerably. Most important is that growth increases value substantially.

Another issue is that the growth rate is quite difficult to estimate and thus subject to substantial measurement error. Small changes in the growth rate can produce large changes in the estimated value. Finally, growth rates change over the life of the company, and so it may be necessary to modify the value estimate based on a variable growth rate.

Moving Beyond Dividends

The ultimate source of value for the shareholder is dividends, present and future. In light of this, you may turn to other sources of value such as EPS (earnings per share), cash flow, revenues, book value or something else, because they may better predict future dividends than do current dividends (which might very well be zero for the company under consideration).

If you use a source of value other than dividends, then it is necessary to estimate the value multiple directly. You can use a number of estimation techniques that we will discuss in Chapter 8. In general there will be a range of multiples that will produce the value range for the stock.

What if You Have Little or No Operating History?

In the case where there is little or no operating history for the company, you may have to use whatever company information is available. A few years ago a company issued stock for the first time (referred to as an *initial public offering* or IPO). The company paid no dividends and had no revenues, assets or even a management team. What, you might ask, is the value of such a company? The market invested $50 million in this IPO! By the way, the company was in the biotech industry, had a board of directors with two Nobel Prize Laureates and a guy who had run a business such as this before. I concluded that the value multiple in this case was $25 million per Laureate!

I say this partly in jest, partly in seriousness, for in situations like this, you can use many different benchmarks. However, in a number of these situations, you have no reasonable way to determine the value of brand-new ventures. In such cases, you may turn to professionals such as venture capitalists to help you identify good opportunities. They have the expertise to analyze start-ups and to size up the company's management.

Should You Visit the Company?

Sometimes investors like to visit with the managers of the companies in which they plan to invest. My own experience is that it is very difficult to get a good feel for management by meeting with them. I have consulted with companies for many years and am still not sure that I have a good feel for the management. I don't know how you can get a good feel during a single, short meeting. Thus I don't believe visiting with management is worth the time and effort.

CONSTANT AND VARIABLE DIVIDEND GROWTH VALUATION

VALUE INVESTING TIPS

▼ Dividends, both present and future, are the primary source of value for the company, so it makes sense, when possible, to base your valuation on dividends.

▼ The constant growth dividend valuation model is easy to use, but the challenge is to estimate the long-term dividend growth rate.

▼ In many situations, you cannot assume a constant growth rate, so it is necessary to apply a variable growth rate model.

▼ You can use the dividend valuation model only for stocks paying a meaningful dividend and most effectively for utility and blue chip stocks.

Focusing on dividends paid seems a logical approach to valuing a stock. Obviously, this approach makes sense only when the company is currently paying a dividend. Thus you cannot use dividend valuation for the many thousands of stocks that are not currently paying dividends. In addition, for companies that pay only a token dividend (roughly stocks with a payout ratio of less than 10 percent), the dividend valuation model is of questionable reliability.

Estimating Growth and the Required Return Are Critical

Your key challenge is estimating the company's growth rate. As we will see shortly, the estimated value is very sensitive to this growth rate estimate. Small changes in the growth rate can produce very large changes in value. In Chapter 8, we will discuss how the growth rate can be more accurately estimated.

The required return for the stock growth rate is another challenging number to estimate. The current Treasury interest rates and a measure of risk for the stock play a role in determining the required return. The difference between the required return and the growth is the only determinant of the dividend value multiple.

Constant Growth Valuation Model

If you assume that dividends will grow at a constant rate for the foreseeable future (actually it is forever), you can estimate the dollar value of the stock as

Equation 7.1:
$$V = DPS/(R - G)$$

Where:
V = current value of the stock

DPS = dividends per share expected to be paid over the next 12 months

R = required rate of return for this particular stock

G = expected constant growth in dividends

When I present this equation in my seminar, someone usually asks why the dividend over the next 12 months is the only dividend being valued. This seems a plausible question because indeed this is the only dividend explicitly shown in the constant growth dividend valuation Equation 7.1. Actually, Equation 7.1 is the result of calculating the value of each and every future dividend, not just DPS over the next 12 months. Because of the particular way the mathematics work out, only DPS for the next 12 months shows up explicitly in the equation. In essence, the value of future dividends are captured by G.

Those who are more mathematically inclined will recognize Equation 7.1 as the closed form solution for the sum of a convergent, geometric series. Those who are not mathematically inclined can ignore what I just said and not miss much that is important.

Another issue regarding Equation 7.1 is the definitions for R and G. R is the required rate of return and can be thought of as the interest rate specific to this particular stock. G, on the other hand, is the expected growth in dividends. These are two very different variables: One is a return on investment; the other is the growth in a cash flow. R is estimated based on market interest rates while G is estimated based on the growth of the company. R is outward looking; G is inward looking.

Estimating DPS

Let's use Equation 7.1 to estimate the value of XYZ Corporation, which was introduced in the previous section as a comparison company for ABC Cruise Lines. To estimate XYZ's value, you have to estimate DPS, R and G. I will assume $0.34 for DPS. I typically use the forecast from *Value Line* or some other investment service without making any adjustments. If such a forecast is not available, I then generate my own forecast of DPS. Estimating DPS is not a major concern because there is not much uncertainty surrounding this number for most companies. Thus I generally do not spend much time refining this estimate.

Estimating R

The starting point for estimating the required rate of return, R, is the risk-free rate as embodied in the current Treasury interest rates. The logic here is that because stocks are risky, you will demand a return that exceeds the return available on risk-free Treasuries. Assume you have looked up the current Treasury interest rates, and they range from 5 percent for 3-month T-bills up to around 6.5 percent for 30-year T-bonds. Since I am looking at a 3-year to 5-year average holding period, I use the five-year T-note rate of 5.5 percent as the risk-free rate.

The next component is a risk premium above and beyond the risk-free rate. Again, because investing in stocks is risky, I want to earn some additional return as a reward for taking on that risk. Over the long run, the typical stock return has exceeded the return on Treasuries by 6 percent. So the required rate of return for the typical case is given by

Equation 7.2: R = Risk-free rate + Risk premium
R = 5.5% + 6% = 11.5%

Thus 11.5 percent is the required return for the typical stock. The required rate of return will change over time as Treasury interest rates change.

Using Beta To Estimate the Required Return

Is XYZ a "typical" stock? There are a number of ways to answer this question. I like to start with the beta for the stock. Beta is a risk measure and is available from a number of investment services, including *Value Line, S&P Stock Reports,* and *AAII Stock Investor. Beta* is easy to interpret in that a value of 1 means that the stock is typical in terms of risk. A beta of greater than 1 means that the stock is riskier than is the typical stock, and a value of less than 1 means that the stock is less risky. More specifically, a beta of 1.5 means that the stock is 50 percent riskier than the typical stock, and a beta of 0.6 means that the stock is 40 percent less risky than the typical stock.

If the market increases by 10 percent, a stock with a beta of 1.5 will increase, on average, by 15 percent. Unfortunately the reverse is also true: A 10 percent market decline will be matched by a 15 percent decline in the stock. The possibility of this latter event, of course, is why beta is a measure of risk.

The beta for XYZ is 0.9; thus XYZ is a little less risky than the typical stock. Beta can be inserted into the equation for R as follows.

Equation 7.3: R = Risk-free rate + (Beta × 6%)
R = 5.5% + (0.9 x 6%) = 10.9%

Thus XYZ's required return is 10.9 percent. This means that if you earn 10.9 percent or higher when you invest in this stock, you will be satisfied. If you earn less, then the stock will have underperformed on a risk-adjusted basis.

Equation 7.3 is the general expression for estimating a stock's required return. Note that R will vary over time as the risk-free rate changes and will vary from stock to stock depending upon the riskiness as measured by beta.

Considerable controversy surrounds beta as a measure of risk. Suffice it to say that many people disagree with my use of beta. But I believe that beta is a reasonable starting point and has the advantage of being widely available. In Chapter 8, I will discuss several other measures of risk that you might consider instead of or as a supplement to beta.

The Sensitivity of Value to Growth Estimates

As we already discussed, the growth rate, G, is the most difficult variable to estimate. In this section, we will explore the sensitivity of V to different estimates of G. In Chapter 8, we will turn the spotlight on a number of growth rate estimation techniques.

XYZ's five-year DPS growth rate is reported in Figure 6.3 as 5.6 percent. If you combine this estimate with the previous estimates of $0.34 for DPS and 10.9 percent for R, the value for XYZ can be estimated as

$$V = DPS/(R - G)$$
$$V = \$0.34/(0.109 - 0.056) = \$6.42$$

Note that both values for R and G are plugged into the equation as fractions and not as percents. So the first estimate of XYZ's value is $6.42.

How sensitive is the value estimate to the estimate of G? Say that you use some other technique and come up with an estimate for G of 10 percent. The value estimate becomes

$$V = \$0.34/(0.109 - 0.10) = \$38$$

Roughly a doubling in G has produced a six-fold increase in V. The value estimate is very sensitive to the growth estimate. This becomes very obvious when the value for G approaches the value for R as is the case above. It is also obvious that growth is *the* major source of value.

In comparison, the no-growth value of XYZ is about $3 (calculated by setting G = 0 in Equation 7.1), so $35 of the $38 of the estimated value (or over 90 percent) is the direct consequence of growth. This is a sobering realization and further motivates you to gain a deeper understanding of XYZ's growth potential. Much of XYZ's value is riding on growth potential.

Let's go a step further and use XYZ's five-year EPS growth rate, reported as 12.8 percent in Figure 6.3, as an estimate for the long-term growth rate in dividends. Using this rate, the value estimate becomes

$$V = \$0.34/(0.109 - 0.128) = \text{undefined}$$

When G equals or exceeds R, the constant growth valuation model breaks down and cannot be used for valuing the stock. In this situation, the stock has to be valued by using the variable growth rate model described next or by using some source of value other than dividends.

Variable Growth Valuation Model

We just saw that when the growth rate equaled 12.8 percent, the constant growth model broke down and the stock could not be valued. What went wrong? The reality is that XYZ cannot grow at 12.8 percent forever. The mathematics of the valuation equation is telling us this because there has never been a stock with an infinite price. Eventually the laws of economics will catch up with XYZ, and its growth rate will slow. This same fate eventually befalls every high growth company. A few years ago IBM was growing at an average rate of 20 percent per year, and no end seemed to be in sight. But suddenly IBM's growth stopped, and new computer powerhouses Intel and Microsoft arose.

The conclusion that a company cannot grow rapidly for a long period was confirmed by a British researcher named I. M. D. Little. In a 1966 book entitled *Higgledy-Piggledy Growth Again,* Little demonstrated that past growth rates are a poor predictor of future growth rates. Thus the name of the book. Little's results, later confirmed by researchers using U.S. data, are the direct result of highly competitive markets both in Britain and the United States in which companies find it difficult to grow rapidly in the face of the entry of new companies and stiff competition.

Two Additional Estimates Required

This argues strongly for valuing stocks using a variable growth rate model. Unfortunately the conceptual appeal of this model is somewhat offset by the added difficulty of estimating two newly introduced variables: the duration of the high growth period and the second stage growth rate. The first issue is the most problematic because it is virtually impossible to predict how long high growth will persist. Beyond the estimation problem, the calculation is more difficult because you now have to determine the present value of each individual dividend separately and then add them together. A computer spreadsheet is a necessity because if you attempt this calculation by hand, you will almost certainly make a mistake.

Figure 7.1 shows the spreadsheet results for XYZ under the assumption that dividends grow at a rate of 12.8 percent for five years and ten years, respectively. After the initial period, growth drops off to the NYSE average of 6 percent (from Figure 6.3). For the five-year high-growth period, the estimated stock value is $9.06 while for the ten-year period it is $11.55.

The most sobering aspect of these estimates is how little additional value is created with five or even ten years of above-average growth. The five-

**FIGURE 7.1 Variable Growth Valuation for
XYZ Corporation ***

Assumed Initial Growth = 12.8%
Second Period Growth   =   6.0
Required Return   = 10.7

Five-Year Higher-Growth Period

Year	Dividend	Value
1	$0.34	$0.31
2	0.38	0.31
3	0.43	0.32
4	0.49	0.32
5	0.55	0.33

Value of dividends year 6 and after	$7.47
Estimated Value of Stock =	**$9.06**

Ten-Year Higher-Growth Period

Year	Dividend	Value
1	$0.34	$ 0.31
2	0.38	0.31
3	0.43	0.32
4	0.49	0.32
5	0.55	0.33
6	0.62	0.34
7	0.70	0.34
8	0.79	0.35
9	0.89	0.36
10	1.01	0.36

Value of dividends year 11 and after	$ 8.20
Estimated Value of Stock =	**$11.55**

*Estimated value for XYZ equals $7.23 if dividend
grows at a constant rate of 6%.

year value is $1.59 greater than the average growth
value of $7.23 while the ten-year period adds
another $2.49 over the five-year value. Given the
unpredictable nature of future growth and the very
long periods necessary to create a significant
increase in value, it is little wonder that "growth"

investing has had such a spotty performance record relative to value investing.

Don't Substitute EPS for DPS in the Variable Growth Model

One final caution about using the variable growth model: You might be tempted to use this model with EPS rather than DPS. In fact because many high-growth companies do not pay dividends, why not just substitute EPS for DPS in Equation 7.1 or in the spreadsheet shown in Figure 7.1?

Keep in mind, however, that dividend valuation is based on valuing cash flowing into your pocket. A portion of earnings, maybe all of earnings, can be retained by the company rather than being paid to investors. Thus the use of EPS in place of DPS in the dividend valuation model leads to a double counting: It counts the entire EPS as being currently received by the shareholder while also counting the future growth resulting from the retention of earnings. You cannot have your cake and eat it too! To value the company based on earnings, you will have to use one of the techniques described in the next section and in Chapter 8.

EARNINGS AND OTHER VALUATION TECHNIQUES

VALUE INVESTING TIPS

▼ When you focus on other than dividends for valuing, it is necessary to estimate value multiples using historical data for the company or multiples for comparable companies.

▼ Generally a range of value multiples is used resulting in a value range for the stock.

▼ The advantage of using historical data is that it provides an estimate of the noise in the market.

▼ Earnings valuation is the most widely used technique, exceeding even the use of dividend valuation, because you can use it for a broader range of stocks.

There are many stocks for which it is difficult if not impossible to assign a value using dividend valuation. This may be because the company is not currently paying a dividend or is paying only a nominal dividend (roughly those stocks with a payout ratio of less than 10 percent). Another reason is that many analysts feel that earnings or some other measure provides a better indicator of future dividends than is the current dividend.

Figure 7.2 shows the distribution of dividend yield and the three-year cumulative EPS from continuing operations for the 6,636 stocks on the *AAII Stock Investor* database. You can see that 4,084 or 61.5 percent of the stocks do not pay dividends, thus dividend valuation cannot be used for these stocks. On the earnings side, 31 percent of the stocks have missing or negative cumulative EPS over the previous three years. This is a preliminary indication that EPS valuation may not be possible for about 30 percent of the stocks, necessitating a focus on another source of value such as cash flow, revenue or book value.

Earnings Valuation Model

The basic equation for earnings valuation is

Equation 7.4: $V = (PE) \times EPS$

A couple of important caveats need to be mentioned at this point. The PE ratio in Equation 7.4 is not the stock's current PE. This is because if you multiply the current PE times the current EPS, you get the current price. You thus conclude that every

FIGURE 7.2 Dividend Yield and EPS Distribution of Stocks

Dividend Yield

Yield	Frequency	% of Total	Cum %
0.0%	4,084	61.5%	61.5%
0.5	171	2.6	64.1
1.0	266	4.0	68.1
1.5	293	4.4	72.5
2.0	336	5.1	77.6
2.5	298	4.5	82.1
3.0	246	3.7	85.8
3.5	190	2.9	88.7
4.0	119	1.8	90.5
4.5	96	1.4	91.9
5.0	70	1.1	93.0
5.5	67	1.0	94.0
6.0	57	0.9	94.8
Above 6%	343	5.2	100.0
Total =	6,636		

Sum of 3 years of EPS-Continuing

EPS	Frequency	% of Total	Cum %
$(10.00)	212	3.2%	3.2%
–	1,881	28.3	31.5
1.00	1,108	16.7	48.2
2.00	986	14.9	63.1
3.00	740	11.2	74.2
4.00	507	7.6	81.9
5.00	356	5.4	87.3
100.00	843	12.7	100.0
Total =	6,636		

Includes all stocks traded on the NYSE, AMEX, Nasdaq National Market and some OTC stocks.

Source: January 31, 1996 version of *AAII Stock Investor*. Used with permission.

stock is correctly priced all the time! Of course this is circular nonsense and so it is necessary to estimate the appropriate PE for the stock. Unlike dividend valuation, in which the value multiple was calculated using estimates of R and G, PE estimates are obtained directly from historical information or by using multiples of comparable companies.

What Determines the PE Ratio

Although the PE is not calculated using estimates of R and G, the PE ratio is affected by these two very important variables nonetheless. As interest rates increase causing R to also increase, the PE ratio will decline. On the other hand, as the company's growth rate increases, so will the PE ratio. These relationships are captured implicitly by the methods used to estimate PE.

For a dividend paying stock, the PE will be smaller than is the dividend multiple given by $1/(R - G)$ in Equation 7.1. The ratio of PE to the dividend multiple will be roughly equal to the company's dividend payout ratio. Some companies, primarily utilities, pay virtually all earnings out as dividends and thus the PE for such a company will be equal the dividend multiple. The details of PE ratio estimation are discussed in Chapter 8.

Estimating EPS

Estimating EPS is not as straightforward as is estimating DPS. Because EPS can fluctuate dramatically from year to year, it is a challenge to estimate it. In addition, there are a number of accounting issues surrounding the reporting of earnings. Although unusual, you may have as many as half a dozen EPS estimates to choose from. And even if you settle on one particular estimate, you always face economic and market uncertainties that may cause future earnings to deviate significantly from expectations.

Thus you will split your time between estimating the appropriate PE ratio and the appropriate EPS. Chapter 9 discusses EPS estimation.

Other Valuation Techniques

Valuation using other sources of value is very similar to earnings valuation. You scale up the source of value, whether it be cash flow, revenues, book value or something else, using the value multiple unique for that source, resulting in a valuation model similar to Equation 7.4. Again, the multiple can be estimated using historical data as well as information from comparable companies. I do not discuss the specific details of these other valuation techniques because they are so similar to the earnings valuation techniques described in detail in Chapter 8.

CHAPTER 8

▼ ▼ ▼

Putting Value Analysis
To Work

VALUE INVESTOR'S CHECKLIST

✓ The first step in a value analysis is to conduct
an industry analysis (Chapter 8).

✓ The second step is to conduct a financial ratio
analysis (Chapter 6), comparing the company to
a close competitor, the industry and the market.

✓ The third step is to estimate a value range based
on dividends (Chapter 7).

✓ You should carefully analyze the growth prospects of the company (Chapter 8).

✓ The fourth step is to value the stock based on
earnings (Chapter 7).

✓ You can estimate the appropriate PE ratio by
using several different techniques (Chapter 8).

✓ You should conduct a careful analysis of earnings (Chapter 9).

✓ The final step is to value the stock based on cash flow, revenues, or book value, if necessary (Chapter 7).

✓ Each investor will focus on different steps depending upon the personal investment style and the characteristics of the particular stock being analyzed.

A COOK'S TOUR OF THE *VALUE LINE INVESTMENT SURVEY*

VALUE INVESTING TIPS

▼ The *Value Line Investment Survey* contains a great deal of information that is useful for conducting a value analysis.

▼ The advantage of the *Survey* relative to a *Standard & Poor's Stock Report* is that it is often more up-to-date, and *Value Line* does more of the analysis for you.

▼ The disadvantage of *Value Line* is that it covers fewer stocks than does *Standard & Poor's*.

▼ If you invest in smaller stocks, the *Standard & Poor's Stock Report* may be your only choice.

I consider the *Value Line Investment Survey* to be one of the wonders of the world, at least of the investing world. If you are not familiar with it, be prepared to be dazzled! If you use it regularly, you have probably gotten used to the tremendous variety of information contained on this single-page summary (see Figure 8.1). No other country has an investment service to rival *Value Line*. I believe that the development of such a worldwide service is a

FIGURE 8.1   Westvaco's *Value Line Survey*

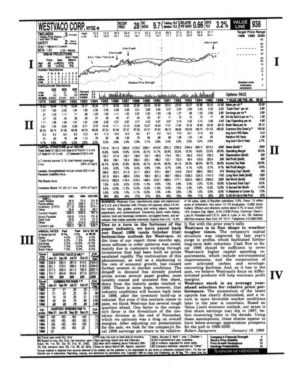

precursor to individual investors managing their own international stock portfolios.

Even though there are many other investment services available, I believe that for most stock investors *Value Line* will be a primary, if not the only, source of investment information. Thus before conducting a value analysis for Westvaco, the company I have chosen as an example, let's take a short tour of the *Value Line Investment Survey* for this company. If you would like to get more information about how to read and use this *Survey*, *Value Line* provides the publication "How to Invest in Common Stocks" to its subscribers (800-833-0046).

Valuation Information for Westvaco

Section I at the top of the *Value Line Investment Survey* in Figure 8.2 contains a preliminary indication of whether or not the stock is undervalued. At the very top is the PE ratio, which is calculated using *centered EPS* or two quarters of the most recently reported EPS added to the next two quarters of projected EPS. This *centered PE* differs from the *trailing PE* reported by most others (and by *Value Line* in the parenthesis), which is based on the most recent four quarters of actual earnings. Thus on average, *Value Line's* PE will be slightly lower than the PE reported elsewhere since for most companies EPS grows over time.

The fact that the current PE of 9.7 is below the *10-year median PE* of 13.0 and the relative PE is 0.66 are preliminary indications that Westvaco is undervalued. The *relative PE* means that the current PE of 9.7 is 66 percent of the *Value Line* median PE, which is currently 14.7 for the roughly 1,700 stock universe followed by *Value Line*. In fact, a low PE is the reason I selected Westvaco for an in-depth analysis. The dividend yield of 3.2 percent is also an indication of undervaluation since it exceeds the market average of 2.2 percent.

Timeliness Rank

Moving down the left side of Section I in Figure 8.2, you come across *Value Line's* proprietary measure of investment attractiveness over the next 12 months, which is called *Timeliness*. It is calculated based on actual data and is heavily influenced by *earnings momentum* (i.e., EPS growth) and *price momentum* (i.e., price appreciation). A stock with strong EPS growth and weak price appreciation will be ranked higher by *Value Line* than a stock with weak EPS growth and strong price appreciation, all other things being equal. *Value Line* does not reveal how they calculate the Timeliness rank because they consider it to be the very heart of their service.

FIGURE 8.2 Westvaco's *Value Line Survey:*
Section I

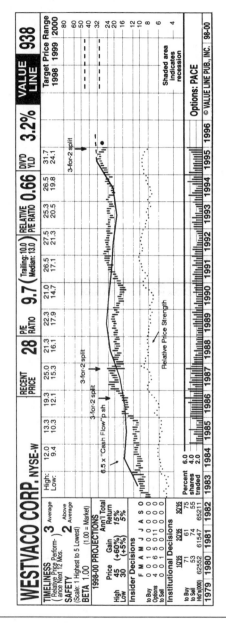

Westvaco with a Timeliness rank of 3 is considered by *Value Line* to be properly valued, at least with respect to the next 12 months. A rank of 1 is the highest rank given while 5 is the lowest. Various studies have shown that *Value Line's* Timeliness rank is a useful tool for identifying undervalued stocks.

A bit disconcerting, however, is that *Value Line's* mutual funds have not performed well. Some argue that this is because *Value Line* has to release the new Timeliness rankings to the public before their own portfolio managers can use this information for trading purposes. Much of the information contained in the new rankings may have already been dissipated by the time *Value Line's* portfolio managers are able to execute their trades. This raises the question of how useful the Timeliness rank is to you even in light of the various studies verifying its benefits.

Three-Year to Five-Year Stock Performance Projections

Continuing to move down the left-hand side of Section I, you come across the 3-to-5 year stock performance projections (titled 1998-00 Projections). *Value Line* is projecting that this stock's price will be from $30 to $45 in the next 3 to 5 years. This translates into an expected annual return from 5 percent to 15 percent. I place more emphasis on this projection than the Timeliness rank because my focus is on the 3-to-5 year time frame and the cash flow valuation underlying these projections.

A graphic representation of this projection is provided in Section I in the form of the two dashed lines at $30 and $45 on the right-hand side of the stock price chart. *Value Line* helps you further by pointing to this range with the dashed line just above the dot which represents the current price of $28.

The *Value Line*

Actually this latter dashed line is the projected path of the *Value Line*, the namesake of the company.

The *Value Line* is *Value Line's* method of determining whether or not the stock is undervalued. For Westvaco, it is created by multiplying 6.5 times the cash flow per share. The cash flow per share is shown on the second line of Section II (Figure 8.3) and is calculated by adding depreciation back to EPS. Like the Timeliness rank, *Value Line* does not explain how it comes up with the 6.5 multiple.

You might compare the price graph in Section I with the value range presented in Figure 4.2. The real world is much messier! The fundamental value of the company does not march upward uninterrupted but takes unexpected turns. The actual price contains much more noise than does the stylistic price series in Figure 4.2. Based on *Value Line,* Westvaco does seem to be undervalued, but because there is not a value range presented in the price chart, it is unclear if this undervaluation is enough to justify purchasing the stock.

In summary, Section I presents a multifaceted picture of Westvaco's value. Unfortunately, not all the arrows are pointing in the same direction. This is almost always the case, so I find it necessary in most situations to do my own analysis beyond that provided by *Value Line.*

Safety Rank

Besides valuation, you will find some very useful information in Section I with respect to the riskiness of Westvaco's stock. *Value Line's* overall measure of risk is the *Safety* rank presented just below the Timeliness rank. The Safety rank also ranges from 1 to 5, with 1 being the safest. Again *Value Line* does not reveal the details on how this rank is determined. Westvaco, with a rank of 2, is above average in terms of safety.

Other Risk Measures

Right below the Safety rank is another risk measure, beta (described in Chapter 7). With respect to beta, Westvaco is an average risk stock.

FIGURE 8.3 Westvaco's *Value Line Survey*: Section II

Sales per sh [A]	14.32	16.44	17.76	16.04	15.77	18.34	17.71	18.59	19.55	22.00	23.43	24.62	23.31	23.45	23.37	25.88	32.22	31.30	*33.50*
"Cash Flow" per sh [A]	1.57	1.80	2.02	1.64	1.66	2.38	2.26	2.36	2.69	3.51	3.89	3.65	3.37	3.20	2.90	3.20	5.03	5.25	*5.80*
Earnings per sh [B]	.91	1.03	1.17	.71	.68	1.29	1.00	1.11	1.35	2.07	2.30	1.93	1.56	1.37	.96	1.03	2.80	2.85	*2.85*
Div'ds Decl'd per sh [C]	.27	.30	.34	.36	.36	.37	.39	.40	.47	.55	.63	.67	.71	.73	.73	.73	.77	.90	*1.00*
Cap'l Spending per sh	1.71	1.68	1.69	1.87	1.97	3.09	3.26	2.57	2.87	3.77	5.43	4.97	3.07	3.19	4.32	2.13	2.86	4.40	*4.80*
Book Value per sh	6.61	7.34	8.04	8.36	8.71	9.72	10.42	11.11	12.10	13.59	15.27	16.53	17.21	17.84	18.18	18.48	20.49	22.15	*26.15*
Common Shs Outst'g [D]	85.50	85.74	87.30	90.39	94.70	96.28	97.24	97.48	97.37	97.00	97.47	97.94	98.73	99.60	100.33	100.75	101.55	102.25	*104.50*
Avg Ann'l P/E Ratio	6.3	6.2	6.4	13.3	9.0	8.4	11.3	13.0	15.0	9.2	8.7	9.2	13.4	17.8	24.1	21.9	9.8		*13.0*
Relative P/E Ratio	.91	.82	.78	.99	1.12	.78	.92	.88	1.00	.76	.66	.68	.86	1.08	1.42	1.44	.65		*1.00*
Avg Ann'l Div'd Yield	4.7%	4.8%	4.6%	5.5%	3.9%	3.5%	3.5%	2.8%	2.3%	2.9%	3.1%	3.8%	3.4%	3.0%	3.2%	3.2%	2.8%		*2.7%*
Sales ($mill) [A]							1721.8	1811.9	1903.6	2133.9	2284.1	2410.8	2301.2	2335.6	2344.6	2607.5	3272.5	*3200*	*3500*
Operating Margin							16.8%	16.8%	19.0%	22.4%	23.1%	21.7%	20.9%	20.2%	18.3%	18.6%	23.5%	*25.0%*	*25.5%*
Depreciation ($mill)							122.7	121.6	129.7	139.9	155.7	169.0	179.4	183.1	195.0	219.3	230.3	*245*	*305*
Net Profit ($mill)							96.6	108.1	132.4	200.4	223.1	188.2	153.1	135.9	96.4	103.6	283.4	*290*	*300*
Income Tax Rate							35.7%	32.0%	37.8%	36.0%	40.1%	42.4%	39.0%	34.1%	29.3%	36.0%	39.7%	*39.0%*	*39.0%*
Net Profit Margin							5.6%	6.0%	7.0%	9.4%	9.8%	7.8%	6.7%	5.8%	4.1%	4.0%	8.7%	*9.1%*	*8.6%*
Working Cap'l ($mill)							338.0	352.3	311.8	317.7	328.2	370.1	309.7	318.9	244.0	269.0	358.3	*410*	*455*
Long-Term Debt ($mill)							501.9	504.4	489.6	576.6	768.0	961.3	969.7	1055.5	1258.3	1234.3	1147.0	*1145*	*1320*
Net Worth ($mill)							1012.9	1082.8	1178.4	1318.3	1488.4	1618.1	1699.5	1777.1	1824.0	1862.0	2080.6	*2265*	*2735*
% Earned Total Cap'l							7.6%	8.4%	9.5%	12.0%	11.4%	9.0%	7.6%	4.8%	5.0%	5.0%	10.3%	*10.0%*	*8.5%*
% Earned Net Worth							9.5%	10.0%	11.2%	15.2%	15.0%	11.6%	9.0%	7.6%	5.3%	5.6%	13.6%	*13.0%*	*11.0%*
% Retained to Comm Eq							5.8%	6.3%	7.4%	11.1%	10.9%	7.6%	4.9%	3.6%	1.3%	1.6%	9.9%	*8.5%*	*7.0%*
% All Div'ds to Net Prof							39%	36%	34%	27%	27%	35%	46%	54%	76%	71%	28%	*32%*	*35%*

Other measures of risk are provided in Section III (Figure 8.4) in the form of the capital structure and the current position. The next section of this chapter will explain these two measures in terms of the financial ratio analysis.

The final risk measures are in the lower right-hand corner of Section IV (Figure 8.5). I can remember the first time I saw this information. As a fellow stock investor, I am sure you would have shared my sense of excitement. The information in this box provides a more detailed picture of the company's riskiness.

Westvaco's *Financial Strength* of A indicates a low default risk. This rating is similar to a Moody's or S&P bond rating of A (the highest *Value Line* rating is A++ compared to AAA for the other two services).

The next three measures are based on a scale of 5 to 100 with 50 being average. Westvaco's stock is above average in terms of *price stability* and about average in terms of *price growth persistence* and *earnings predictability*. I know of no other service that provides such detailed risk information.

Westvaco's risk picture is more consistent than it was for valuation; it seems to be of lower risk and somewhat safer than the average stock.

Insider Decisions

Insiders (as defined by the SEC) are required by law to report their purchase and sale of the company's stock. The information reported on the left-hand side of Section I is a summary of the reports to the SEC. (Insiders are barred from taking a short position in their own stock. Any guesses why?) When interpreting this information, remember that there are many reasons for selling a stock (poor future prospects, college expenses, buying a second home, etc.) but there is only one reason for purchasing a stock: The purchaser thinks the price is heading up. So typically there are more insider sell decisions than buy decisions.

FIGURE 8.4 Westvaco's *Value Line* Summary: Section III

CAPITAL STRUCTURE as of 10/31/95
Total Debt $1188.2 mill. **Due in 5 Yrs** $111.5 mill.
LT Debt $1147.0 mill.   **LT Interest** $100.0 mill.

(LT interest earned: 5.7x; total interest coverage:
5.4x)   (36% of Cap'l)

Leases, Uncapitalized Annual rentals $22.4 mill.
Pension Liability None

Pfd Stock None

Common Stock 101,551,211 shs.   (64% of Cap'l)

CURRENT POSITION (\$MILL.)	1993	1994	10/31/95
Cash Assets	56.6	75.0	151.8
Receivables	225.3	269.4	311.4
Inventory (LIFO)	271.8	236.0	274.1
Other	55.6	50.2	49.7
Current Assets	609.3	630.6	787.0
Accts Payable	100.8	110.0	131.6
Debt Due	30.8	41.6	41.2
Other	233.7	210.0	255.9
Current Liab.	365.3	361.6	428.7

ANNUAL RATES of change (per sh)	Past 10 Yrs.	Past 5 Yrs.	Est'd '93-'95 to '98-'00
Sales	4.0%	2.5%	4.5%
"Cash Flow"	5.0%	-1.5%	9.0%
Earnings	2.5%	-10.0%	12.5%
Dividends	7.5%	6.0%	6.0%
Book Value	7.5%	6.0%	6.5%

Fiscal Year Ends	QUARTERLY SALES (\$ mill.) A Jan.31	Apr.30	Jul.31	Oct.31	Full Fiscal Year
1992	539.8	593.4	587.9	614.5	2335.6
1993	561.1	579.5	586.0	618.0	2344.6
1994	577.3	626.4	641.3	762.5	2607.5
1995	741.7	804.6	854.6	871.6	3272.5
1996	765	800	800	800	3200

Fiscal Year Ends	EARNINGS PER SHARE A B Jan.31	Apr.30	Jul.31	Oct.31	Full Fiscal Year
1992	.27	.41	.36	.33	1.37
1993	.21	.20	.32	.32	.96
1994	.16	.16	.20	.51	1.03
1995	.49	.65	.79	.88	2.80
1996	.60	.65	.75	.85	2.85

Cal-endar	QUARTERLY DIVIDENDS PAID C Mar.31	Jun.30	Sep.30	Dec.31	Full Year
1992	.183	.183	.183	.183	.73
1993	.183	.183	.183	.183	.73
1994	.183	.183	.183	.183	.73
1995	.183	.183	.183	.22	.77
1996	.22				

FIGURE 8.5 Westvaco's *Value Line Survey:* Section IV

BUSINESS: Westvaco Corp. manufactures paper and paperboard at 5 U.S. and 2 Brazilian mills. Primary mill capacity: about 2.8 million tons/year. Key grades: printing and writing papers, bleached paperboard, and containerboard. Converting plants make folding cartons, food and beverage containers, corrugated boxes, and envelopes. Also makes specialty chemicals. Exports from U.S.: 13.2%

of '94 sales, sales of Brazilian subsidiary: 5.8%. Owns 1.5 million acres of timberland. Has about 14,170 employees, 13,890 shareholders. Officers and directors control about 5.7% of stock; ESOP, 12%, Invesco Cap. Mgmt., 9.4% (12/95 Proxy). Chairman: David L. Luke III. President and C.E.O.: John A. Luke, Jr. Inc.: DE. Address: 299 Park Avenue, New York, NY 10171. Telephone: 212-688-5000.

Due to a turn in the fortunes of the paper industry, we have pared back our fiscal 1996 (ends October 31st) bottom-line outlook for Westvaco. At the time of our report three months ago, some softness in order patterns was noted, mainly due to customers working through inventories that had been built as prices escalated rapidly. The continuation of this phenomenon, as well as a slackening in the rate of economic growth, has caused further erosion in market conditions. The dropoff in demand has already pushed prices across several paper grades, most notably coated and uncoated free sheet, down from the historic peaks reached in 1995. There is some hope, however, that industry conditions will bounce back later in 1996, after the inventory build-up is reduced. But even if this scenario comes to pass, we think Westvaco has several tough quarters ahead. One factor in the company's favor is the divestiture of the container division at the end of November, which we estimate was a drag on overall margins. After adjusting our presentation for the sale, we look for the company's fiscal 1996 earnings per share to be relative-

ly flat with the prior year's tally. **Westvaco is in fine shape to weather tougher times.** The company's capital structure was improved by last year's surge in profits, which facilitated further long-term debt reduction. Cash flow in fiscal 1996 should be sufficient to cover Westvaco's higher capital spending requirements, which include environmental improvements, and the construction of new activated carbon and envelope-converting facilities. And, as it has in the past, we believe Westvaco's focus on differentiated products will help maintain profit margins.

Westvaco stock is an average year-ahead selection for relative price performance. The momentum of the latest upcycle has clearly diminished, and a return to more favorable market conditions later in the year is uncertain. Based on Value Line's economic outlook, our sense is that share earnings may dip in 1997, before recovering later in the decade. Using these assumptions, these shares appear to have below-average appreciation prospects for the pull to 1998-2000.

Robert Jacapraro   *January 19, 1996*

Company's Financial Strength	A
Stock's Price Stability	85
Price Growth Persistence	50
Earnings Predictability	50

To subscribe call 1-800-833-0046.

(A) Fiscal year ends Oct. 31st.
(B) Based on avg. shs. Excl. nonrecur. gain (loss): '84, 1¢; '95, 12¢; '87, 21¢; '91, (24¢); '93, 23¢; extraord. loss: '93, 11¢; '95, 2¢. Qtrly. EPS may not sum to total due to rounding. Next earnings report due about February 28th. Goes ex about March 5th. Approx. payment dates: January 3, April 1, July 1, October 1.
(C) Next dividend meeting about February 28th.
(D) In millions, adjusted for stock splits.
(E) Company estimate, reported as "Other".

Even though there is a considerable lag between the date of the insider trade and the date it is reported in *Value Line* (note that this summary is dated 1/19/96 while the most recent insider information is for October 1995), a number of studies confirm the usefulness of this information in predicting subsequent returns. For example, the large number of options exercised during the middle of 1995 was a strong indication of insider buying and was a positive sign for Westvaco stock. This was followed by several months of no insider activity, preceding the late year stock price decline.

Insider Ownership

Insider holding information is provided in the top right of Section IV (Figure 8.5). Reading the *Business* section reveals that officers and directors control about 5.7 percent of the stock while the ESOP (employee stock ownership plan) owns about 12 percent. The total insider ownership of about 18 percent is within the 10 percent to 20 percent that many feel is ideal.

Institutional Ownership

Institutional ownership (e.g., mutual funds, banks, pension plans, insurance companies and so forth) of Westvaco stock is quite high at 64 percent (calculated as the third quarter 1995 institutional holdings from the left-hand side of Section I [Figure 8.2] divided by 1995 shares outstanding from the seventh line in Section II [Figure 8.3]). I generally stay away from such high institutional ownership (the median is 52 percent for the NYSE). High institutional ownership usually attracts considerable analyst coverage, and that makes it less likely the stock will be undervalued. I like to find undervalued stocks before the institutions do.

When an institution or individual purchases more than 5 percent of the shares outstanding, it must report this position to the SEC. Note that in the upper right corner of Section IV (Figure 8.5)

Invesco Capital Management has amassed a 9.4 percent stock position in the company. You may find it useful to learn why Invesco took this position. Such large positions are neither good nor bad in themselves.

Historical Financial Data

Section II (Figure 8.3) and Section III (Figure 8.4) contain a substantial amount of financial data for the company. Up to 15 years of income statement and balance sheet data is displayed in Section II. All share information is adjusted for stock splits and stock dividends so that you need not be concerned with these events. You will notice that Westvaco had two stock splits, both three-for-two splits, one in 1986 and another in 1987.

Various studies have shown that stock splits have no predictive power in terms of future price performance. Adjusting share information to eliminate their effect is the right way to handle stock splits and stock dividends.

Financial Projections

One of *Value Line's* attractive features is the projected numbers shown on the right-hand side of Section II (Figure 8.3). Both one year ahead and three-year to five-year projections are provided. Like any other projection, there is a degree of uncertainty surrounding these estimates. With a value of 50 for earnings predictability (lower right corner of Section II), Westvaco projections contain an average level of forecast error. The financial data and forecasts in Section II will be used in the value analysis of Westvaco that follows.

Capital Structure

Section III (Figure 8.4) contains additional information about Westvaco's financial condition. The capital structure box at the top of Section III gives a quick picture of the long-term financial structure for the company. It is composed of 36 percent long-term bonds and 64 percent stock with no preferred stock. In addition, there are no pension liabilities and minimal uncapitalized leases. Under current accounting practices most long-term leases must be capitalized (i.e., the present value of the future lease obligations) and treated as long-term debt. If you are a conservative investor, the capital structure box will be of greater interest to you.

Current Position

Moving down Section III (Figure 8.4), the current position box provides recent and historical information about the company's current assets and liabilities (maturity of less than a year). I do not spend much time on this information, but again if you are a conservative investor, this box will be of interest.

Growth Rates

The next box in Section III (Figure 8.4) shows both ten-year and five-year historical as well as 3-to-5 year projected growth rates for a number of key financial series. This information is used extensively in the value analysis that follows. *Value Line* saves you a considerable amount of time by providing an array of calculated and projected growth rates.

The last three boxes in Section III display five years of actual and projected quarterly sales, EPS and DPS.

Qualitative Information

Section IV (Figure 8.5) contains the qualitative information, including detailed information about the company in the *business* section at the top of the section and a 400-word analyst report in the lower portion. This section provides background information about the company as well as the future direction of the industry and the company in the opinion of Robert Jacapraro, the *Value Line* analyst for Westvaco. Sometimes you will notice the analyst disagreeing with the "black box" Timelines rank for the company. For Westvaco, this does not seem to be the case. The very bottom boxes summarize some of the most important footnotes from various annual reports.

INDUSTRY ANALYSIS

VALUE INVESTING TIPS

▼ You must understand the company in the context of the industry in which it operates.

▼ At the end your analysis, you should have an understanding of three things about the industry: (1) the profitability drivers, (2) the current situation and (3) the future prospects.

The current state of the industry within which the company operates is a major factor underlying the current state of the company. There are many sources of information about the industry, ranging from the one-page *Value Line Industry Summary* to the longer *S&P Industry Outlook* to the much longer industry reports available from various brokerage firms. I will focus on the *Value Line Industry Summary* because of its brevity and timeliness.

How Did You Get Here Anyway?

Before diving into the details, you might very well ask how I got to the point of doing an industry analysis. There are two possible routes, each equally plausible. In one, you might have identified the paper & forest products industry as an attractive industry in terms of Timeliness, PE, the current point in the business cycle or some other criteria that you read or heard about. You want to conduct a thorough analysis of the industry to determine if your initial impression is right. If it is, you will then select the best stock in this particular industry. If you are following this particular route, you will probably want to go beyond the single page *Value Line Industry Summary*.

By the second route, you will have identified Westvaco as a stock of interest and now want to learn something about the industry in which it operates. This is the route that I followed. Since my focus is more on individual stock selection, I generally don't go beyond the brief industry report provided by *Value Line*.

Which Industry?

While there is a generally agreed upon industry classification, you will find that different investment services will classify the same company in different industries. For example, *Value Line* classifies Westvaco in the paper & forest products industry, one of 96 separate industries identified by *Value Line*. *AAII Stock Investor*, on the other hand, classifies Westvaco in the paper & paper products industry, one of 103 AAII industries. Forestry and wood products is a separate industry in the AAII classification. Thus as you move from service to service, be aware that the company you are analyzing may be reclassified into a different industry and the membership of the industry itself might change.

Value Line Industry Summary

Figure 8.6 shows the *Value Line Industry Summary* for the paper & forest products industry. In studying this summary, try to answer three questions: (1) What are the profitability drivers for the companies in this industry? (2) What is the current state of this industry? and (3) What are the future prospects for this industry? Let's address these questions one by one using the industry summary in Figure 8.6.

What Are the Profitability Drivers for Companies in This Industry?

Each industry has a different set of economic and competitive forces that shape the industry and determine which companies will thrive and which will wither. Understanding these forces is very useful when you begin the value analysis for a particular company.

Although I am focusing on the material presented in the *Value Line Industry Summary* in Figure 8.6, it may not always be possible to satisfactorily answer this question by simply reading this one-page summary. You may need to read more extensively about the industry in order to obtain a complete picture of the competitive landscape in the industry. General business publications such as *The Wall Street Journal, Barron's, BusinessWeek, Fortune* and *Forbes* are good sources of such information.

What can you surmise about this industry from Figure 8.6? First of all, this is a "commodity" type industry, which means that it is very difficult for a particular company to differentiate its product from everyone else's product. Companies in such industries compete mainly on price. It is very difficult to charge a price higher than your competition, and the low cost provider dictates the price level.

The intensity of competition shows up in the *% Earned Net Worth* (other services call it ROE), six rows up in the financial table in the lower left corner of the summary (Figure 8.6). Until recently this number has hovered around 3 percent for this industry, very poor by most standards. As we will learn shortly, the recent dramatic increase in ROE to around 20 percent is the result of dramatic increases in paper prices during 1995. This feature is a bit worrisome because individual companies have little influence over paper prices in this highly competitive and seemingly overcapacity industry.

FIGURE 8.6 *Value Line Industry Summary*

January 19, 1996   **PAPER & FOREST**

Our outlook for the paper industry is becoming increasingly pessimistic. Instead of a temporary inventory correction, we now believe that prices for most grades likely peaked in the fourth quarter and that demand will not pick up significantly, if at all, in coming months. Meanwhile, lumber prices should move slightly higher.

Lower prices

Paper and Board Pricing

Since the summer of 1994, the industry has enjoyed its most rapid recovery in history. However, it appears in retrospect, that the dramatic price gains enjoyed by most grades were made possible in part by tremendous inventory accumulation in the first half of 1995. This has led to substantial downtime at numerous mills, which are hoping to keep prices from falling by reducing production. Although list prices haven't dropped significantly, if at all, in the cases of newsprint and groundwood papers, there has been widespread discounting in numerous markets as manufacturers seek to preserve market share. Among the grades witnessing the greatest declines are linerboard, corrugating medium, pulp (especially hardwood), and, on the paper side, the lighter coated paper grades, as well as uncoated free sheet to a lesser extent.

-high inventory -Lower prices

The AFPA Survey

The *American Forest & Paper Association's* annual capacity survey released last month states that industry capacity additions will gather momentum in the coming three years. Total paper and paperboard capacity, which was expected to grow annually by 1.9% according to last year's report, will rise by 2.5% annually out to 1998. Because virtually all paper and paperboard markets have enjoyed extraordinary success over the past 18 months, many companies initiated small capital projects to achieve maximum production. As a result, the manufacturing base figures for 1994 and 1995 were moved upward. This revision suggests that operating rates for most paper grades were somewhat beneath the level once estimated. Hence, the markets were a little less tight than previously thought, and thus vulnerable to softer pricing.

Capacity up

In particular, the paperboard side of the business is expected to see the fastest rate of capacity additions, or 3.3% annually. A slew of announcements earlier last year pushed the rate for printing and writing papers up to 2.4%. Meanwhile, newsprint, tissue, and packaging papers are all expected to rise by less than 1%.

Paperboard strong

Composite Statistics: PAPER & FOREST PRODS. INDUSTRY

1991	1992	1993	1994	1995	1996		98-00
88500	91346	93504	99647	138650	145000	Sales ($mill)	177500
12.2%	12.1%	12.4%	14.6%	19.5%	18.7%	Operating Margin	18.0%
5714.8	6241.3	6444.4	6572.4	8300	8800	Depreciation ($mill)	10300
1373.1	1160.9	1235.9	3123	9800	9700	Net Profit ($mill)	12000
44.1%	35.7%	36.9%	38.1%	36.8%	37.1%	Income Tax Rate	37.3%
1.6%	1.3%	1.3%	3.1%	7.1%	6.7%	Net Profit Margin	6.8%
5500.2	4817.5	6131.0	6682.7	10000	10600	Working Cap'l ($mill)	18000
35345	36452	37777	37430	36000	34000	Long-Term Debt ($mill)	40500
42128	41137	40688	43885	49000	57500	Net Worth ($mill)	84000
4.0%	3.5%	3.6%	6.5%	15.0%	14.0%	% Earned Total Cap'l	10.0%
3.3%	2.8%	3.0%	7.0%	20.0%	18.0%	% Earned Net Worth	14.0%
NMF	NMF	NMF	3.0%	15.0%	13.0%	% Retained to Comm Eq	8.0%
122%	NMF	NMF	53%	25%	25%	% All Div'ds to Net Prof	25%
41.1	NMF	NMF	24.4	*Bold figures are*		Avg Ann'l P/E Ratio	10.0
2.63	NMF	NMF	1.60	*Value Line*		Relative P/E Ratio	.75
3.0%	2.6%	2.4%	2.3%	*estimates*		Avg Ann'l Div'd Yield	3.0%

Factual material is obtained from sources believed to be reliable, but the publisher is not responsible ...fidential use of subscribers. Reprinting, copying, and distribution by permission only. Copyright 1996 by

FIGURE 8.6 *(Continued)*

Investors may want to concentrate on companies with exposure to these latter grades, while avoiding liner-board and corrugating medium, the two primary reasons for paperboard's relatively unpromising outlook.

avoid liner-board and corrugate

Lumber Profits Should Improve Slightly
The markets endured another volatile year in 1995, as the first-half decline in pricing was sharply reversed by a pickup in housing construction in June. However, seasonal weakness in the fourth quarter applied further pressure to prices, which are roughly 10%-15% below year-ago levels at present.

Lumber prices ↓ 10-15%

On balance, we think lumber companies will see better earnings this year. The onslaught of Canadian lumber imports (which account for over a third of all softwood lumber sold in the U.S.) that suppressed domestic mills' profits seems to have abated in recent months. Higher imports were not only a function of our dollar's relative strength but, more importantly, also the integrated Canadian companies' need for fiber (wood chips are a byproduct of log production) to supply their booming paper operations. Canadian sawmills continued to cut logs for chips, despite cheap lumber prices. Domestic producers have recently complained that they are at a disadvantage because the Canadian Government subsidizes the forestry industry by allocating timber rights rather than promoting bidding as in the U.S. As we went to press, it looked as though negotiations between the Canadian and U.S. Governments will lead to the British Columbia and Quebec provinces revising their pricing schedules to avoid a trade war.

In sum, with housing starts expected to remain level along with mortgage rates, and log costs slightly less expensive, we think that the profitability of lumber companies will improve by the second quarter.

Lumber improving

Investment Advice
In spite of the industry's favorable Timeliness rank, we would encourage investors to be cautious regarding their positions in paper-related issues. The rash of analyst downgrades since the third quarter has left many stocks with seemingly cheap valuations. Still, we feel that the newly revised capacity forecast and present inventory situation in most grades point to softer pricing in coming quarters.

many analyst downgrade

Charles C. Moran

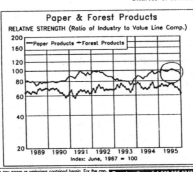

Paper & Forest Products
RELATIVE STRENGTH (Ratio of Industry to Value Line Comp.)
— Paper Products — Forest Products
Index: June, 1967 = 100

What Is the Current Situation in the Industry?

As we just saw, 1995 was a very good year for the paper & forest products industry because paper prices rose dramatically. In fact, 1995 was one of the industry's best years in history. But by the end of 1995, there were already signs that prices were weakening. In addition, most companies took the opportunity to expand capacity, setting the stage for an industry faced with overcapacity.

Figure 8.6 provides some information about the lumber market, but because Westvaco does not produce lumber, we will ignore it.

What Are the Future Prospects for the Industry?

Charles Moran of *Value Line* is suggesting that the industry will be able to hold onto some recent gains but that overcapacity is a serious problem. In terms of individual products, paperboard is very strong while liner board and corrugate are weak. Moderate growth is expected over the near term. This is an industry clearly at the mercy of the business cycle.

Industry Timeliness

In the upper right corner (Figure 8.6), you will find the *Industry Timeliness* rank; it is calculated by averaging the timeliness rank of all the companies in the industry and then ranking all industries based on their average timeliness. This industry is ranked 34th out of 96, which means that it is an above-average industry in terms of timeliness.

Industry Financial Data

In the lower left corner (Figure 8.6) is the composite financial information for the industry, presented in the same format as the lower part of Section II (Figure 8.3) in the *Value Line Investment Survey*. This section will be the source of the industry benchmark in the financial ratio analysis presented in the next section of this chapter.

Industry Relative Strength

In the lower right corner (Figure 8.6) is a graph of the industry's relative strength. *Relative strength* is measured as the average stock price appreciation of the companies in this industry divided by the average price appreciation for all of the 1,700 stocks in the *Value Line* universe, multiplied by 100. June 1967 was set to equal 100, so you can see that the stock performance of the paper & forest products industry has been virtually identical to that of the market because the industry's Relative Strength is currently about 100.

FINANCIAL RATIO ANALYSIS

VALUE INVESTING TIPS

▼ A financial ratio analysis allows you to quickly determine if further analysis effort is warranted.

▼ The ratio analysis for Westvaco reveals that growth potential is an area of concern but profitability is quite strong.

▼ The valuation ratios indicate a potential undervaluation while the financial structure ratios are acceptable.

The financial ratio analysis for Westvaco is presented in Figure 8.7. Besides benchmarks for the paper & forest products industry and the NYSE, Figure 8.7 contains benchmarks for Mead Corpora-

FIGURE 8.7 Financial Ratio Analysis for Westvaco

Ratio	Westvaco	Mead	Paper & Forest Products Industry	NYSE
5-Year Earnings Growth	–10.0%	–19.0%	32.0%	6.0%
5-Year Dividend Growth	6.0%	3.3%	–7.0%	3.2%
Net Profit Margin (earnings/ revenues)	8.7%	4.9%	7.1%	5.8%
Return on Equity (ROE) (earnings/share- holder equity)	13.6%	11.9%	20.0%	12.0%
Price to Earnings (PE) ('94)	21.9	19.9	24.4	16.5
Price to Book (PB) ('94)	1.4	1.4	1.7	1.9
Dividend Yield ('94) (DPS/ price)	3.2%	2.0%	2.3%	1.1%
Current (Current Assets/Current Liabilities)	1.8	1.7	?	1.6
Long-Term Debt to Capital (capital is sum of long-term debt, preferred stock, share- holder equity)	36%	25%	42%	33%

Source: *Value Line Investment* and *Industry Summaries* except for NYSE medians, which were obtained from 1/31/96 edition of *AAII Stock Investor*.

tion, a similarly sized paper products firm. The ratios, with the exception of those for the NYSE, are drawn from or calculated using data from the *Value Line Investment Survey* in Figures 8.1–8.5 and the *Value Line Industry Survey* presented in Figure 8.6. To help you find information in the *Value Line Investment Survey* in Figures 8.1–8.5, the location (e.g., Section I, II, III, or IV) is shown after each number.

Of course it is not necessary to use *Value Line* summaries for conducting a ratio analysis. Any number of other investment information services can supply the needed data. A number of these services provide the ratios directly, and some services can be directly tied to spreadsheets or other software packages that automatically calculate the desired set of ratios.

You can obtain the NYSE (or another market) averages from a number of sources such as *The Wall Street Journal, Barron's, Value Line* and *Investor's Business Daily.*

Growth

The growth rates in Figure 8.7 reveal a confused picture for Westvaco. The five-year EPS growth rate (Section III, Figure 8.4) for both Westvaco and Mead are negative and substantially below the industry and market growth rates. I calculated the industry growth rates using the financial data in the *Industry Summary.* On the other hand, the five-year DPS growth rate (Section III) picture looks much stronger with Westvaco exceeding all three benchmarks. A confused growth picture is not that unusual, so you will often conduct a more thorough analysis of the company's growth potential. The next section in this chapter will focus on this.

Profitability

Unlike growth, Westvaco's profitability measures are quite strong in Figure 8.7. The net profit margin (Section II, Figure 8.3) exceeds all three other benchmarks. The most relevant comparisons are to Mead and the industry because net margins differ widely from industry to industry. Westvaco's ROE (Section II) exceeds all but the industry benchmark. It is legitimate to compare ROE to the industry as well as to the market.

Valuation

The valuation ratios provide an initial indication of whether or not Westvaco is undervalued. In fact, I used the PE ratio as a screening criteria for identifying this stock for further investigation. The PE ratio presented in Figure 8.7 does not appear to be that attractive relative to the three benchmarks (recall that a lower PE is preferred). The reason I chose 1994 is that it is the latest year for which there is an industry benchmark. Westvaco's current PE is a much more attractive 9.7 (Section I, Figure 8.2). Finding comparable benchmarks can be a problem whenever you are constructing a financial ratio analysis such as that presented in Figure 8.7. Use your best judgment when making such comparisons so that the benchmarks are truly comparable.

Both the price to book ratio (calculated using data from Section I, Figure 8.2) and the dividend yield (Section I) provide an indication of undervaluation. The PB for Westvaco is less than or equal to the three other benchmarks while the DY is higher. These results combined with the now much lower PE send a clear signal that this stock is worth further investigation.

Financial Structure

The final area on which you focus is Westvaco's financial structure. Both the current ratio (calculated using data from Section III, Figure 8.4) and the long-term debt-to-capital ratio (Section III) indicate an acceptable financial structure. Note that the industry's current ratio cannot be calculated from the data in the *Value Line Industry Summary*.

A company's financial structure can be a deal killer but not a deal enhancer. That is, you might very well discard a stock because you feel the company has taken on too much debt, but it is highly unlikely that a stock will increase in attractiveness simply because of a low amount of debt. Put another way, an acceptable financial structure is a necessary but far from sufficient reason for investing in the stock.

Overall Impression of Westvaco

You will have to piece together the disparate parts of the ratio analysis to develop an overall impression of the stock. Bringing together the various elements leads me to conclude that Westvaco is worth further consideration. The growth picture is confused, profitability is strong, valuation is attractive and the financial structure is acceptable. So I would move onto the next step in the value analysis.

PROFITABILITY AND GROWTH ANALYSIS

VALUE INVESTING TIPS

▼ Both profitability and growth are important determinants of value.

▼ You can gain an understanding of how a company generates its ROE (return on equity) by conducting a Dupont ratio analysis.

▼ ROE plays a central role in estimating the company's sustainable growth rate.

▼ Examining the growth rate at various stages in the production process provides insight into how the company is performing.

▼ The profitability and growth analysis for Westvaco indicates a weak future growth potential while raising the concern that current strong profitability may be transitory.

Note: To help you find information in the *Value Line Investment Survey* in Figures 8.1–8.5, the location in the *Survey* (e.g., Section I, II, III, or IV) is shown after each number.

A ratio analysis generally does not give you enough information concerning the company's profitability and growth potential. Therefore, you should dig further into these two very critical determinants of value. Now I know you may be saying to yourself that you already know more than you ever wanted to know about Westvaco. But trust me when I tell you that you need to know more!

Remember that your goal is not to identify the profitability and growth stars of tomorrow but to have a good handle on the true profitability and growth potential for the company so that you can value the company correctly. You are willing to buy a low-profitability and low-growth company as long as the price is right.

Profitability Analysis

An examination of Westvaco's net profit margin (Section II, Figure 8.3) and ROE (Section II) reveals a dramatic improvement in 1995 as compared to the previous four years. What do you make of this newfound prosperity? You need to answer this question before proceeding with your valuation.

A *Dupont ratio analysis* is useful for answering this question. It allows you to break down Westvaco's ROE into three components as

Equation 8.1:

$$ROE = NPM \times TAT \times EM$$

Where: ROE = return on equity (Section II, earnings/equity)

NPM = net profit margin (Section II, earnings/revenues)

TAT = total asset turnover (Section II and other, revenues/total assets)

EM = equity multiplier (Section II and other, total assets/equity)

FIGURE 8.8 Dupont Analysis for Westvaco

Ratio	1993	1994	1995
Net Profit Margin (NPM) (Earnings/Revenues)	4.1%	4.0%	8.7%
Total Asset Turnover (TAT) (Revenues/ Total Assets)	0.60	0.65	0.77
Equity Multiplier (EM) (Total Assets/Equity)	2.20	2.10	2.00
Return on Equity (ROE)* (NPM × TAT × EM)	5.4%	5.5%	13.4%

*Differs from ROE reported in *Value Line* due to rounding.

Source: *Value Line Investment Survey* and 1/31/96 edition of *AAII Stock Investor*.

You cannot obtain total assets from the *Value Line Investment Survey*, so to calculate both the TAT and the EM, you will have to obtain the company's total assets from another source such as *S&P Stock Reports* or *AAII Stock Investor*.

Figure 8.8 presents Westvaco's Dupont analysis for the three years 1993, 1994 and 1995. The NPM shows a very strong improvement in 1995 as compared to the two earlier years. The narrative by Robert Jacapraro (Section IV, Figure 8.5) confirms that 1995 was an extraordinary profit year. But on the unsettling side, Charles Moran in the *Industry Summary* points out that many companies in the industry have increased capacity during the year thus making it problematic whether the 1995 NPM can persist in the face of overcapacity. Given the commodity nature of the industry, I would say that future margins will decline from their 1995 levels.

The TAT shows a very healthy trend over the last three years, increasing from $0.60 of revenue for every dollar of assets to $0.77. To the extent that this improvement is the result of the 1995 price increase, this higher TAT may not be sustainable in the future. However, there does seem to be some good news here since the TAT improved from 1993 to 1994 prior to the 1995 price increase.

Equity Multiplier

The final component of the Dupont analysis is the equity multiplier (EM). This measures the impact of Westvaco's use of debt financing on profitability. Using debt per se cannot make a firm profitable. Instead debt, with its fixed interest payments, amplifies the return to shareholders. This can be either good or bad. If the company's NPM is negative, then the return to shareholders is even more negative because the interest payments have to be made to debt holders. On the other hand, if NPM is positive, the return to shareholders is magnified by the EM.

This latter case is much like the situation you face as a homeowner with a large mortgage when housing prices increase and as a result your equity in the house increases severalfold. For example, if you have taken out a 90 percent mortgage on a $100,000 house and prices go up by 10 percent, your equity doubles from $10,000 to $20,000 or a 100 percent increase. Note that in this case your EM is 10 ($100,000/$10,000) and the house appreciation of 10 percent has been amplified by 10, that is, from 10 percent to 100 percent. The EM plays the same amplifying role in Equation 1 for the company.

Westvaco's EM as shown in Figure 8.8 has declined about 10 percent over the last three years. This means that the company has decreased its use of debt relative to equity financing and thus its financial structure has gotten more conservative. Most investors would view this as a positive trend. This makes the company less vulnerable to an economic downturn.

Putting this all together, you can see that Westvaco's profitability has improved over the last three years. All three of the components have moved in the right direction over this time period. The one major concern is whether the company will be able

FIGURE 8.9   Actual and Projected Growth Rates for Westvaco

Financial Series	Past 5 Years	Projected 3–5 Years
Shareholder Equity	6.0%	6.5%
Revenues	2.5%	4.5%
Earnings per Share	–10.0%	12.5%
Dividends per Share	6.0%	6.0%

Source: *Value Line Investment Survey.*

to maintain the high 1995 NPM in the face of over capacity in this commodity type industry.

Growth Analysis

We now turn to the second important value determinant, the company's growth potential. As a starting point, we will focus on the actual and projected growth rates for Westvaco presented in Figure 8.9. I have arranged these rates in this particular order because they provide additional insight into the growth profile of the company.

How does a company grow? First, it retains earnings for reinvestment in the company. This retention shows up as growth in shareholder equity, the first item shown in Figure 8.9. The company then invests the retained earnings in assets, both physical and human, ultimately producing more revenues. This is the second item in Figure 8.9. Revenue growth provides the basis for earnings growth, which is the third item. Finally, from earnings dividends are paid. Thus Figure 8.9 presents a growth chronology for Westvaco.

The past five years show mixed results. Shareholder equity has grown an average of 6 percent annually, but revenues have expanded at a mere 2.5 percent rate, while EPS actually declined over the period. DPS did grow at the same rate as did shareholder equity. The three-year to five-year projections are a bit more positive with EPS growing much faster than shareholder equity. But these are only projections, so they are subject to error.

What would be an ideal growth profile? In general, you would expect revenues to grow faster than shareholder equity and in turn EPS to grow faster than revenues. Both of these faster growth rates would be the result of productivity gains in the company: more revenue per dollar of assets and in turn more profit per dollar of revenue. For a typical company, you should observe revenues growing 1 percent to 2 percent faster than shareholder equity and EPS growing 1 percent to 2 percent faster than revenues. You are not so concerned about the DPS unless it exceeds EPS growth which is obviously not sustainable over the long run. On the other hand if DPS is growing slower than EPS the company's ability to pay future dividends is improving, very much a positive turn of events.

Sustainable Growth

Most companies, with the exception of rapidly growing small companies, do not issue new shares into the market. This seems to be the case for Westvaco, as can be seen from its history of shares outstanding (Section II, Figure 8.3). Thus for the vast majority of companies the only way to grow is to retain earnings, invest these into new company assets and manage these assets so that new revenues and earnings result. *Sustainable growth*, then, is the rate at which the company can grow through the retention of earnings without the issuance of new shares. This internally generated growth rate is given by

Equation 8.2: $\qquad G_S \qquad = \text{ROE} \times \text{Retention ratio}$

$\qquad\qquad$ Where: $G_S \qquad = $ sustainable growth rate

$\qquad\qquad\qquad$ ROE $\quad = $ return on equity

$\qquad\qquad\qquad$ Retention $= $ fraction of ratio $\qquad$ earnings retained

FIGURE 8.10 Sustainable Growth Rates for Westvaco

Variable	1993	1994	1995
Return on Equity (ROE) (Earnings/Equity)	5.3%	5.6%	13.6%
Retention Ratio 1 − (DPS/EPS)	0.24	0.29	0.72
Sustainable Growth (G_S) (ROE × Retention Ratio)	1.3%	1.6%	9.8%

Source: *Value Line Investment Survey.*

Westvaco's sustainable growth rate is reported in Figure 8.10 for the three years 1993 through 1995. The retention ratio is calculated by subtracting the payout ratio (last line in Section II, Figure 8.3) from 1. For example, the payout ratio for 1993 was 76 percent, so the retention ratio is 1 − 0.76 = 0.24. Multiplying ROE by the retention ratio yields an estimate for G_S. Westvaco's sustainable growth potential exploded upward in 1995.

Much of this improvement can be traced back to the very strong industrywide prices during 1995. Higher prices led to wider profit margins, which in turn produce stronger profitability and higher sustainable growth. Though you are pleased to see the stronger growth potential, you need to keep in mind the difficulty Westvaco may have in maintaining a high net profit margin in this commodity type industry.

DIVIDEND VALUATION

VALUE INVESTING TIPS

▼ You should value the company based upon the dividends being paid whenever possible.

▼ Obviously if the company is not paying a dividend, dividend valuation models cannot be used.

▼ A company paying only a token dividend is also not a good candidate for application of the dividend valuation model.

▼ I apply this model to Westvaco and find that the stock is overvalued.

Note: To help you find information in the *Value Line Investment Survey* in Figures 8.1–8.5, the location in the *Survey* (e.g., Section I, II, III, or IV) is shown after each number.

Now we are finally ready to get to the heart of value investing, that is, the estimation of a value range for Westvaco. Let's estimate the first value range based on dividends being paid. We will incorporate much of what we covered in the previous sections in developing the value range.

Constant Growth Valuation

Constant growth dividend valuation model was introduced in Chapter 7 and is

Equation 8.3: V = DPS/(R – G),

Where: V = current value of the stock

DPS = dividends per share expected to be paid over the next 12 months

R = required rate of return

G = expected constant growth in dividends

For Westvaco, I use the 1996 projected dividends of $0.90 (Section II, Figure 8.3) for DPS.

The required return is: R = risk-free rate + (beta × market risk premium) = 5.5 percent + (1 × 6 percent) = 11.5 percent, where 5.5 percent is the current 3-year to 5-year Treasury interest rate, 1 is Westvaco's beta (Section I, Figure 8.2) and 6 percent is the historical market risk premium.

The growth rate is the most difficult variable to estimate. To guide us in selecting the right value for G, we will use some of the analysis presented in Section D above. The initial estimate for G is drawn from the actual and projected growth rates presented in Figure 8.9 (Section III, Figure 8.4). The appeal of this array of growth rates is that it captures growth at various stages in the production process and is both backward and forward looking. This latter point means that we are using a *centered growth rate estimate*, in the same vein as *Value Line* uses a "centered" PE ratio. Again, our ultimate goal is to obtain the best estimate of Westvaco's long-term dividend growth potential. The initial estimate is obtained by averaging the 8 growth rates in Figure 8.9 to yield 4.3 percent.

Generally at this point in my seminar, participants object to the seemingly arbitrary nature of this calculation. I respond that estimating G is equal parts art and science and that the above technique does have a plausible basis. However, there are many ways that the growth rates in Figure 8.9 can be combined to come up with an estimate for G. Feel free to develop your own unique approach.

Putting these estimates together, the initial value estimate is

$$V = DPS/(R - G)$$
$$V = \$0.90/(0.115 - 0.043) = \$12$$

This is less than half the current price of $28 (Section I, Figure 8.2).

We obtain the next estimate by averaging the four projected growth rates in Figure 8.9 and using the resulting 7.4 percent in Equation 1.

$$V = \$0.90 / (0.115 - 0.074) = \$22$$

This value estimate is higher but is still less than the current price of $28. I am less confident in this estimate because it is based exclusively on projected growth rates.

Sustainable Growth Valuation

Figure 8.10 presented the estimated sustainable growth rates for Westvaco. Using the three growth rates of 1.3 percent, 1.6 percent and 9.8 percent in Equation 8.3, we obtain value estimates of $9, $9 and $53, respectively. This is a very wide range indeed! Again given the difficulties faced by Westvaco in maintaining those high 1995 margins, the soundness of the $53 estimate is in doubt.

The Market's Growth Expectation for Westvaco

It should be obvious at this point that coming up with a growth rate estimate is a significant challenge. Let's turn this question around and ask what growth rate the stock market is expecting from Westvaco. This question can be answered by substituting the current price for V in Equation 8.3 and solving for G_M, the stock market's growth rate expectation.

$$V = DPS / (R - G_M)$$

and rearranging:

Equation 8.4: $G_M = R - (DPS/V)$

$$G_M = 0.115 - (\$0.90/\$28) = 8.3\%$$

Note that G_M is equal to Westvaco's required return net of the dividend yield. I have taken the liberty of converting G_M to a percentage figure.

Focusing on G_M provides a different perspective on the growth issue. Is the 8.3 percent growth rate market expectation achievable by Westvaco? It is aggressive from the point of view that the average NYSE stock growth rate is only 6 percent. Is it possible for a commodity type company to experience above-average growth? I have a hard time believing that this is possible.

Next you might ask what net profit margin is necessary in order to sustain this level of growth? If you tie together Equation 8.1 for ROE and Equation 8.2 for G_S, the net profit margin NPM_M necessary to sustain the market's growth rate expectation is

Equation 8.5: NPM_M = $G_S/(TAT \times EM \times$ Retention rate)
$$NPM_M = 8.3\%/(0.77 \times 2.00 \times 0.72) = 7.5\%$$

That is, for Westvaco to sustain an average growth rate of 8.3 percent, it has to maintain a net profit margin of 7.5 percent. Westvaco's average NPM over the 11 years for which *Value Line* (Section II, Figure 8.3) provides data is 6.8 percent. Therefore, I conclude that the market's current growth rate expectation for Westvaco is unrealistic and the stock is overvalued at a price of $28.

The Value Range

We have generated a number of value estimates for Westvaco stock. How do you now go about creating a value range? Let's use the first estimate of $12 as the lower bound for the value range. Two of the sustainable growth estimates were lower, but I believe they are unrealistically low. Let's take the second estimate of $22 as the upper bound. The growth rate of 7.4 percent, upon which this estimate is based, is sustainable assuming Westvaco is able to maintain its historical 6.8 percent NPM. The other higher estimates do not seem reasonable in light of the competitive pressures facing Westvaco. Therefore, the value range is $12 to $22, and I conclude that the stock is currently overvalued.

EARNINGS VALUATION

VALUE INVESTING TIPS

▼ Earnings valuation is the most widely used valuation technique.

▼ When valuing earnings, you have to estimate the appropriate PE using actual data.

▼ The value range that I estimate based on earnings indicates that Westvaco is at the lower end of its value range.

Note: To help you find information in the *Value Line Investment Survey* in Figures 8.1–8.5, the location in the *Survey* (e.g., Section I, II, III, or IV) is shown after each number.

Many more stocks have earnings than pay dividends. For this reason and others, earnings valuation is the popular valuation technique. In addition, many analysts believe that earnings are in some sense more fundamental than are dividends.

High and Low PE Valuation

The stock price for a company gyrates over time. Sometimes these movements are the result of the arrival of new information, but many times the price movement cannot be explained by changes in fundamentals and so such movements are referred to as noise. The stock's noise level is the major determinant of the width of the resulting value range. By examining the high and low PE ratios in each of the previous years, you can measure the normal level of noise in the stock.

Figure 8.11 displays the high and low PEs for Westvaco for each of the five years 1989 through 1992 and 1995. I exclude 1993 and 1994 because

FIGURE 8.11   High and Low PEs for Westvaco

PE	1989	1990	1991	1992	1995	Average
High	10	11	17	20	11	14
Average	9	9	13	18	10	12
Low	8	8	11	16	9	10

Source: *Value Line Investment Survey.*

they are the two highest PE years during the most recent 17 years (Section II, Figure 8.3). I choose this particular time period because it is long enough to capture a complete business cycle, but not so long as to obscure a fundamental change in the market valuation of Westvaco's earnings. The annual average PE ratio is reported directly in *Value Line* while the high and low PEs are calculated using the reported high and low prices (Section I, Figure 8.2) and the reported EPS (Section II, Figure 8.3). You can avoid doing this calculation by looking up the high and low PEs in Westvaco's *S&P Stock Report.*

Using the averages from Figure 8.11, you will obtain the value range:

$$\text{High V} = 14 \times \$2.80 = \$39$$
$$\text{Average V} = 12 \times \$2.80 = \$34$$
$$\text{Low V} = 10 \times \$2.80 = \$28$$

I used the 1995 EPS (Section II, Figure 8.3) for valuation. Note that this value range is higher than is the one we estimated using dividends. In fact the two value ranges do not overlap. This happens more frequently than you might think. We will address this issue at the end of this chapter.

Relative PE Valuation

As we saw in Chapter 5, the average PE for the market as a whole varies over time. Thus it makes sense to take into account these market-wide changes by calculating a relative PE ratio. You can do this by dividing Westvaco's PE by the market's

FIGURE 8.12 Relative PEs for Westvaco

	1989	1990	1991	1992	1995	Average
Relative PE	0.66	0.68	0.86	1.08	0.65	0.79

Source: *Value Line Investment Survey.*

PE. Figure 8.12 displays the relative PE ratios for the time period 1989–92 and 1995.

Because the market is being represented by the *Value Line* universe, you need to use the median *Value Line* PE in order to estimate the value based on relative PE. If you are using some other investment information service you will have to use the appropriate market index. By the way, I am unaware of any other service that reports historical relative PEs. So if you plan to use this valuation method you may be limited to using *Value Line.*

Based on the average relative PE of 0.79 reported in Figure 8.11, the estimated value is

$$V = \text{Relative PE} \times \text{Market PE} \times \text{EPS}$$
$$V = 0.79 \times 15.4 \times \$2.80 = \$34$$

where 15.4 is the median *Value Line* market PE ratio reported on the front cover of the *Value Line Weekly Summary.* This estimate is in the middle of the value range presented above.

Graham and Dodd Earnings Valuation

Benjamin Graham and David Dodd along with Sidney Cottle are referred to as the fathers of securities analysis. While I am not as conservative as this threesome, I have the utmost respect for their unique investment style.

A number of years ago, Graham and Dodd conducted some empirical tests to determine the relationship between a company's growth rate and its PE. They estimated this relationship as

$$PE = 8.5 + 2G$$

That is, if the company is not growing, the PE ratio should be 8.5 and increase at double the growth rate if there actually is growth. The problem with this equation is that for the time period over which the tests were run, there were stable interest rates. Of course, recent years have witnessed dramatic interest rate changes, so the equation has to be modified to capture them. A few years ago a modified Graham and Dodd equation was proposed as

Equation 6:   PE   = $(8.5 + 2G) \times (4.4/AAA)$
                Where: AAA = current AAA
                            Corporate Bond
                            interest rate
                   4.4% = the average AAA
                            Corporate Bond
                            rate over the time
                            period of Graham
                            and Dodd's study

Plugging in a conservative 6 percent for G and the current AAA rate of 7.10 percent, the estimated PE is

$$PE = (8.5 + 2(6)) \times (4.4 / 7.10) = 13$$

and the resulting value is

$$V = 13 \times \$2.80 = \$36$$

Again this is in the middle of the initial value range.

Value Range

The estimated values based on earnings provide a consistent picture. The earnings value range is $28 to $39, and the current stock price of $28 is at the very bottom of this value range.

OTHER VALUATION TECHNIQUES

VALUE INVESTING TIPS

▼ Valuation based on cash flow per share, revenues per share and book value per share are often quite useful in valuing smaller stocks.

▼ Like you did for earnings valuation, high and low value multiples are calculated for each valuation approach.

▼ Applying these techniques to Westvaco shows that the stock is correctly valued.

Note: To help you find information in the *Value Line Investment Survey* in Figures 8.1–8.5, the location in the *Survey* (e.g., Section I, II, III, or IV) is shown after each number.

Cash Flow per Share Valuation

Beyond earnings valuation, many analysts prefer to use cash flow valuation because it avoids the distorting effects of noncash items, mainly depreciation. Again, cash flow per share (Section II, Figure 8.3) is calculated by adding depreciation per share to EPS. As we saw earlier in this chapter, the *Value Line* (Section I, Figure 8.2) estimated by *Value Line* for Westvaco is based on cash flow per share, scaled up by a 6.5 multiple. According to this calculation as shown in Section I of Figure 8.2, Westvaco is undervalued.

Panel A in Figure 8.13 displays the high and low price to cash flow ratios for the five years 1989–92 and 1995. The data used for calculating these ratios is presented at the bottom of Figure 8.13. The averages and estimated value were calculated in the same manner as they were in the EPS valuations.

FIGURE 8.13 Other Valuation Techniques for Westvaco

A. Valuation Based on Cash Flow per Share

Price/ Cash Flow	1989	1990	1991	1992	1995	Average	Estim. Value*
High	5.7	5.8	7.9	8.6	6.3	6.8	$34
Low	4.6	4.0	5.1	6.7	4.8	5.0	$25

*Based on 1995 cash flow per share of $5.03

B. Valuation Based on Revenues per Share

Price/ Revenues	1989	1990	1991	1992	1995	Average	Estim. Value*
High	0.95	0.85	1.14	1.17	0.98	1.02	$32
Low	0.76	0.60	0.73	0.91	0.75	0.75	$23

*Based on 1995 revenues per share of $31.30

C. Valuation Based on Book Value per Share

Price/ Book Value	1989	1990	1991	1992	1995	Average	Estim. Value*
High	1.46	1.27	1.54	1.54	1.55	1.47	$30
Low	1.17	0.89	0.99	1.19	1.18	1.09	$22

*Based on 1995 book value per share of $20.49

Data Used for Calculating the High and Low Ratios

	1989	1990	1991	1992	1995
High Price	$22.30	$21.00	$26.50	$27.50	$31.70
Low Price	17.90	14.70	17.10	21.30	24.10
Cash Flow Per Share	3.89	3.65	3.37	3.20	5.03
Revenues Per Share	23.43	24.62	23.31	23.45	32.22
Book Value Per Share	15.27	16.53	17.21	17.84	20.49

Source: *Value Line Investment Survey.*

You can see that the value range is from $25 to $34, implying that the stock is properly valued.

Revenue and Book Value Valuation

In a similar manner, panels B and C in Figure 8.13 display the multiples and value ranges for revenue per share and book value per share valuations, respectively. For consistency, I have again eliminated 1993 and 1994 from the analysis. The value ranges for both of these techniques indicate that Westvaco is correctly valued at $28 per share.

WELL, IS THE STOCK UNDERVALUED?

We have followed a long route in our value analysis of Westvaco. So what have we learned? Westvaco is a paper products company that competes in a commodity type industry. The year 1995 was an exceptionally good one for the industry, with paper prices increasing dramatically and profit margins nearly doubling from 1994 levels. The profitability, value and financial structure ratios all look positive for Westvaco.

Growth is problematic, however. A careful analysis reveals that Westvaco's sustainable growth rate is not sufficient to meet the market's growth expectation implicit in the current price of $28. The value range based on dividends confirms this. Figure 8.14 shows that the value ranges based on earnings, cash flow, revenues and book value are all higher than the dividend-based value range.

Based on the value analysis, I conclude Westvaco is correctly valued at $28 and does not represent an attractive buy opportunity at this time. If I currently own this stock, should I sell it? A reasonable case can be made for selling the stock, particularly in light of the growth analysis and the dividend valuation. But I also think holding onto the stock would be reasonable. There just is not an overwhelming sell signal at this point.

A couple of final comments are in order before we close the chapter on Westvaco. You might have been asking yourself why I picked such a boring stock to analyze: a paper products company. But the truth is that if you pursue value investing, you will spend a great deal of time analyzing similarly boring companies. A value investor analyzes boring stocks because that is often where the value is. If following what is currently "hot" is your desire, value investing is not for you.

The other question you might have been asking yourself is this: Isn't there a shortcut to value analysis? I did go through a very thorough analysis of Westvaco, and the answer to whether or not the

FIGURE 8.14   **Value Ranges for Westvaco**

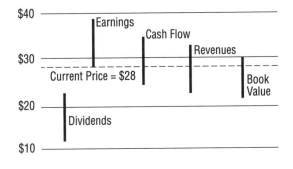

stock should be purchased wasn't clear until close to the end. Somewhat frustrating was the fact that the initial indication, based on the valuation ratios, was that Westvaco was undervalued. But as we moved through the detailed analysis, it became clearer that the stock was correctly valued to maybe even overvalued. This is the nature of the quest. Stocks that initially look good when subjected to a coarse screen can turn out to be flawed when put through a finer screen. It is not always necessary to conduct a full analysis on every stock, for some will drop out in the early stages. But the full range of techniques should be kept at the ready if the need arises.

CHAPTER 9

▼ ▼ ▼

Taking a Closer Look at Earnings

VALUE INVESTOR'S CHECKLIST

✓ You will sometimes have to take a closer look at reported earnings to ensure that they are the best possible representation of the company's earning power.

✓ Major issues revolve around restructurings, acquisitions, mergers, spinoffs, write-downs and restatements of past earnings.

✓ Recently many companies have taken charge-offs and write-downs, some as often as annually.

✓ You may have difficulty deciding in these situations whether you should use the reported EPS (earnings per share) or the EPS from continuing operations or some other measure.

✓ Starting in 1996, companies began to comply with SFAS 121 that allows company write-downs of "impaired" assets, further reducing the quality of earnings.

✓ Beyond the accounting uncertainties, EPS is always subject to economic and market uncertainty.

✓ You should consider a range of EPS estimates when valuing earnings.

ACCOUNTING ISSUES FOR REPORTED EPS

VALUE INVESTING TIPS

▼ Reported EPS is subject to a number of interpretations of accounting rules, including writedowns, acquisitions, mergers, spinoffs, restructuring and restatement of previous earnings.

There are a wide range of accounting issues that, when interpreted in different ways, lead to wildly different reported EPS (earnings per share). These interpretations are generally within the "wiggle room" allowed by accounting standards and are generally not the result of bad faith efforts by management. This makes it necessary for you to become your own accounting detective.

Even if there is not an issue surrounding how the numbers should be reported, you may still have to decide whether the adjustment made by management is appropriate for you as a potential investor. This issue usually takes the form of trying to determine whether you should use the reported EPS or the EPS from continuing operations or some other estimate. This often is not an easy decision.

Things Are Getting Worse

Below we will analyze one of the most extreme accounting situations I have ever seen, the 1993 financial statements for American Cyanamid. But before we dive into these statements, I want to emphasize that, if anything, the confusion surrounding reported earnings will get worse in the near future. Already a number of companies have been charging off restructuring expenses, some as often as every year.

Starting in 1996 a new accounting standard—SFAS 12—set by the Financial Accounting Standards Board (FASB) allowed companies to charge off any *impaired asset*. These assets, for one reason or another, are judged to be underperforming, and they are *charged off* by including their value as an expense item in the income statement. Furthermore, the company is allowed to group assets as they choose, charging off poorly performing individual operating units while doing nothing with stronger units. This further reduces the quality of reported earnings. If this accounting change turns out to be as disastrous as it appears, you may have to abandon EPS entirely and focus instead on cash flow or net free cash flow for valuation purposes.

The Opposing Views of Investors and FASB

Why is the FASB doing this to us investors? Because FASB is balance-sheet oriented while stock investors are income-statement oriented. The non-cash write-offs improve the quality of the balance sheet while destroying the quality of reported EPS. From an investor perspective, this seems a silly trade-off, but unfortunately it is now a reality.

The American Cyanamid Example

In 1993, American Cyanamid (AC), a large pharmaceutical company, issued financial statements that involved virtually every quality-destroying variation known to the accounting profession. The resulting impact was so great that AC reported a 1993 loss of $12.44 per share compared to the previous year's profit of $4.35. This represented accounting housecleaning on a grand scale. Subsequently the company was taken over by American Home Products at the end of the 1994 at a price that was twice the then market price, so the company no longer exists independently. What a profitable housecleaning, at least for the investors!

If you go through the same analysis described below, you would need to consult the footnotes to the financial statements contained in the annual report. I do not provide the details of these footnotes below, only my interpretation of them.

Effects of Acquisitions on Reported EPS

AC's 1993 income statement is displayed in Figure 9.1. The first accounting issue encountered is the acquired in-process research and development (R&D) expenses of $383.6 million. During 1993 AC acquired a 54 percent stake in Imunex, a biotech company. The accounting effect was to increase operating expenses by the amount of acquired R&D expenses and a small earnings impact of –$8.9 million for the minority interest in Imunex owned by outsiders. Overall, the acquisition strongly depressed AC earnings due to the very large R&D expenses and little revenue from Imunex.

Another possible acquisition effect is that if AC paid more than book value for Imunex, the difference, oddly referred to as "goodwill," would be depreciated over time. Thus the acquisition may have further depressed earnings because of higher depreciation.

Restructuring

In some respects, restructuring charges represent one of the most challenging accounting issues for investors. AC's $207.9 million restructuring charge represents, in all likelihood, the cost of laying off employees (severance pay, early retirement payments and other outplacement expenses). The problem is that if you eliminate this charge

FIGURE 9.1 1993 Income Statement for American Cyanamid (AC)

(Millions of dollars except per share amounts)

Years ended December 31,	**1993**	
Net Sales	$4,276.8	
Expenses:		
Manufacturing cost of sales	1,632.9	
Selling and advertising	1,306.8	
Research and development	595.6	
Administrative and general	300.5	
Acquired in-process research and development (Note 3)	383.6	—Imunex
Restructuring (Note 3)	207.9	acquisition
	4,427.3	
Earnings (loss) from operations	(150.5)	Layoffs
Interest and other income, net	100.7	– severance pay
	(49.8)	– early retirement
Interest expense	62.4	
Earnings (loss) before taxes on income	112.2	
Taxes on income (Note 9)	42.6	
Earnings (loss) before minority interests	(154.8)	
Minority interests	(8.9)	—Imunex (46%)
Earnings (loss) from continuing operations	(163.7)	
Discontinued operations (Notes 2,8,9 and 12):		
Earnings (loss) from operations, net of taxes	(75.6)	—Spinoff of Cytex (Chemical)
Loss on distribution, net of taxes of $44.2	(326.8)	
Cumulative effect of accounting changes, net of taxes of $144.9	(219.8)	—Past retirement benefits
	(622.2)	
Earnings (loss) before cumulative effect of accounting changes	(785.9)	
Cumulative effect of accounting changes (Notes 9 and 12)	(332.6)	
Net earnings (loss)	$(1,118.5)	
Per share of common stock (Note 1):		
Earnings (loss) from continuing operations	$ (1.82)	
Earnings (loss) from discontinued operations	(6.92)	
Earnings (loss) before cumulative effect of accounting changes	(8.74)	
Cumulative effect of accounting changes	(3.70)	
Net earnings (loss)	$ (12.44)	

Source: American Cyanamid 1993 annual report. Used with permission.

when estimating EPS, you run the risk of overstating EPS. This is of particular concern when a company restructures on a regular basis, as some have done in recent years. You worry about the company throwing out its dirty laundry in the restructuring garbage bag.

Taxes

The IRS does not follow the same set of accounting rules for determining taxable income as does the FASB. This is quite obvious, for AC's taxable income reported in the income statement is $112.2 million while taxes paid is $42.6 million. Apparently the IRS did not agree with all of AC's write-offs since AC ended up paying taxes even though it reported negative taxable income. You need to be aware that accounting income can differ significantly from IRS taxable income.

Discontinued Operations

During 1993 AC spun off Cytec, their agricultural chemical business. A spinoff means that AC shareholders were asked to swap their existing AC shares for a package containing a share in the remaining AC and a share in Cytec. They were then free to sell one or both shares if they so chose. The accounting adjustment triggered by this swap was the $75.6 million operating loss, the $326.8 million loss on distribution and the $219.8 million accounting change. AC decided to realize the entire loss within the remaining AC enterprise rather than in the newly independent Cytec. Where the loss is realized is of little concern to existing shareholders because they end up owning both entities. But for new investors, this decision further depressed earnings for the residual AC stock.

Accounting Changes

If things are not confusing enough, from time to time the FASB changes the way certain items are accounted for and asks companies to restate past earnings and report the cumulative effect on the current financial statements. This is why AC is reporting an additional loss due to accounting changes of $332.6 million. This change was the result of the FASB requiring companies to charge off post-retirement benefits immediately rather than waiting until they were actually incurred. In theory, this should have no impact on the company's profitability because the company is committed to paying these expenses. But charging them off all in one year had a dramatic negative impact on 1993 earnings. Many other companies ran into this same issue in the early 1990s.

WHICH EPS DO YOU USE?

The American Cyanamid example I just described presents you with the dilemma of which EPS to use. The EPS reported by the company was a loss of $12.44. Certainly you would not use this estimate in AC's value analysis because it badly understates AC's earning power. Turning to the investment services, AC's *S&P Stock Report* showed 1993 EPS as the loss from continuing operations of $1.82. Again, I don't believe this is a useable number since it is distorted by the Imunex acquisition and the restructuring charge. *Value Line* reported a 1993 EPS of $3.87! They removed all of the one-time accounting adjustments and then threw in another $1.55 per share for good measure. I was not able to replicate their estimate using the information from AC's income statement.

So which one do you use? I chose to use the *Value Line* estimate of $3.87 per share, but I was not completely comfortable with this number due to the phantom $1.55. In situations like this, you will have to exercise judgment in selecting the EPS estimate for valuation purposes.

Economic and Market Uncertainty

Even if you are able to resolve all of the accounting issues, you still face economic and market uncertainties about the appropriate EPS estimate to use. Many analysts follow companies very closely and provide earnings forecasts, which represent a good starting point for incorporating economic uncertainty into your value analysis. Earnings forecasts are available from the *Value Line Investment Survey,* the *Standard & Poor's Stock Report* and *AAII Stock Investor.* Other services provide earnings forecasts as well.

In early 1994, *Value Line* was projecting a 1994 EPS of $4.00 for AC; *Standard & Poor's* was projecting $4.25; and *AAII Stock Investor,* which summarizes information from I/B/E/S, an earnings projection reporting service, was showing an EPS range of $4.00 to $4.35. You can use this range to augment your value range calculations.

For example, you can calculate the *highest-high value* and the *lowest-low value* by multiplying the highest PE by the highest projected EPS and the lowest PE by the lowest projected EPS, respectively. You can use these extreme values to modify your value range. However, there are times when I conclude that these values are too extreme and stay with my original value range.

Earnings Predictability

A final way to appreciate the degree of economic uncertainty for a particular company is to consider *Value Line's* Earnings Predictability measure in the right-hand corner of Section IV, Figure 8.5. This measure ranges from 100 (highly predictable) to 5 (unpredictable). AC had an Earnings Predictability measure of 90 in early 1994, so EPS uncertainty due to economic and market uncertainty is not a major concern for AC. On the other hand, this measure was 50 for Westvaco, implying that EPS uncertainty is much more of an issue for this company. For example, the I/B/E/S range reported for

Westvaco in *AAII Stock Investor* for 1996 EPS is $2.40 to $3.50. This is wide enough to consider modifying the earnings value range we estimated in Chapter 8.

CHAPTER 10

▼ ▼ ▼

Some Final Thoughts

From the economy to the industry to financial statements to value ranges, we have explored all of the important ideas and techniques underlying value investing. I am sure that at times you were excited and at other times confused, although the latter will diminish as you adapt these techniques for managing your own stock portfolio.

I want to assure you that success is yours for the taking. By spending a few hours each month on value investing, you can create a winning portfolio. And to help you get off on the right foot, keep the following in mind.

The Art and Science of Value Investing

I have tried to be as explicit as possible in describing the techniques of value investing. Where possible, we have examined real-life examples of how each technique can be applied. But in applying these techniques to your own portfolio, you will have to add a fair measure of judgment. Each stock is different and thus requires a different level of emphasis on the various techniques we discussed.

In the final analysis, your buy and sell decisions will be based on a number of analytical results that will often be in conflict with one another. Over time you will develop a thoughtful as well as flexible set of decision rules.

The Three Secrets of Successful Value Investing: Patience, Patience and More Patience!

You will master the techniques of value investing, but if you don't stick with them over time, you will gain nothing from all the extra effort. It is very difficult to stick with something that is not currently working. Every time you look at your portfolio you are painfully reminded of this failure. But the loud and clear message of history is that value investing does not work with each and every stock and in each and every year; it *does* work in every lifetime. If your goal is to have the maximum amount of money in your portfolio at some future date, then value investing is worth sticking with through thick and thin.

Don't Fall into the Popularity Trap

I never cease to be amazed at how many people want to invest in that which is familiar to them. If they purchase brand-name stocks, people feel much more comfortable with their portfolios. But one of the important messages of value investing is that such stocks are less likely to be values and that the unfamiliar and boring stocks are more likely to be values. By deciding to be a value investor, you are dedicating your portfolio life to the analysis of boring, little-known and at times downright scary stocks. But what you give up in current acceptance and satisfaction, you gain in long-term superior performance.

The Investor's Blessing

Finally, I want to leave you with the investor's blessing: May you always buy low and sell high! Good investing!

APPENDIX

▼ ▼ ▼

Value Investing Resources

A great deal of information is available to help you implement your particular value investing program. This section highlights only those resources that I have personally found, through experience, to be useful.

For General Investment Information

Barron's. This weekly sister to *The Wall Street Journal* focuses on investing, and it provides less general economic information. (800-544-0422)

Investor's Business Daily. This weekday newspaper focuses on the stock market. Espouses a growth investing philosophy. (800-831-2525)

U.S. Financial Data. This weekly publication reports money supply and interest rate information published by the St. Louis Federal Reserve Bank. (314-444-8808)

The Wall Street Journal. This widely respected newspaper is an excellent source of information about the economy and markets as well as individual industries and companies. Published Monday through Friday, it does not espouse any particular investment style. (800-778-0840)

Wall Street Journal Interactive Edition. This is the Internet version of *The Wall Street Journal.* The information is updated very frequently and is available 24 hours a day. One of the very attractive features is the briefing books available for thousands of companies. (http://wsj.com)

For Individual Stock Information

AAII Stock Investor. A floppy disk-based computer program that provides hundreds of items on over 6,600 stocks. Updated every three months. (312-280-0170)

Standard & Poor's Stock Reports. An investment service that provides individual reports for many thousands of individual companies. S&P covers more stocks than does *Value Line,* but the S&P is not as thorough nor as up-to-date as is the corresponding *Value Line Investment Survey.*

Value Line Value Screen. A floppy disk-based computer program that covers the same stocks as does the *Investment Survey.* Can be updated as often as you wish but does not contain all the information included on the hard copy *Investment Survey* version of a report. (800-833-0046)

Value Line Investment Survey. An investment service that covers 1,700 stocks, updated on a rolling 13-week cycle. Excellent source of information on individual stocks. *Value Line* also publishes a supplemental service that covers an additional 1,800 stocks with less frequency. (800-833-0046)

For Further Reading in Value Investing

Financial Statement Analysis: Theory, Application, and Interpretation by Leopold A. Bernstein (Irwin; Burr Ridge, Illinois). A thorough treatment of how to understand and analyze financial statements.

The Intelligent Investor by Benjamin Graham (Harper Collins, New York). An excellent description of the basis of value investing. Ben Graham is considered one of the fathers of value investing.

International Investments by Bruno Solnik (Addison Wesley Publishing Company). The first and most carefully researched book dealing with the advantages of investing internationally. Presents the case for diversifying internationally.

Stocks for the Long Run: A Guide to Selecting Markets for Long-Term Growth by Jeremy J. Siegel (Irwin; Burr Ridge, Illinois). Provides an excellent historical perspective of stock market performance as well as the relative performance of both growth and value investing.

Organizations Providing Investment Education

American Association of Individual Investors (AAII). 625 North Michigan Avenue, Chicago, Illinois 60611; 312-280-0170.

National Association of Investors Corporation (NAIC). Umbrella organization for investment clubs. P.O. Box 220, Royal Oak, Michigan 48068; 810-583-6242.

National Council of Individual Investors (NCII). 1900 L St., NW, Suite 610, Washington, DC 20036; 202-467-6244.

Glossary

▼ ▼ ▼

ADR American depositary receipt. A way to purchase shares of foreign companies by purchasing receipts issued against a deposit of foreign stock. Traded on U.S. exchanges, many on the NYSE.

beta A measure of a stock's riskiness. A beta of 1 means that the stock is of average risk.

book value per share Shareholder equity divided by the number of shares outstanding.

capital structure The composition of the long-term financing of a company such as long-term debt, preferred stock and common stock.

cash flow Earnings plus noncash items, mainly depreciation.

constant growth dividend valuation model Valuing a stock based upon the assumption that dividends grow at a constant rate into the foreseeable future. Can be used only if the company is paying dividends.

current assets Company assets with a maturity of less than one year.

current liabilities Company obligations with a due date of less than one year.

current ratio Current assets divided by current liabilities. A measure of the company's liquidity and of more importance to conservative investors.

DPS Dividends per share.

dividend yield DPS divided by the stock price.

EM Equity multiplier, total assets divided by shareholder equity.

EPS Earnings per share.

fundamental value The economic value of the stock based upon the monetary flows of the company.

growth investing An investment style that tries to identify the growth stocks of the future.

IPO Initial public offering of a company's stock.

long-term debt-to-capital ratio   The ratio of long-term debt to the total capital (e.g., long-term debt, preferred stock and stock) of the company.

market-to-book ratio   Market price per share divided by book value per share.

Nasdaq   National Association of Security Dealers Automated Quotations. Computer trading system for the so-called over-the-counter (OTC) stock market.

neglected stocks   Stocks that receive very little analyst coverage. Tend to be smaller stocks.

net income   Earnings or profits of the company, calculated as revenues net of all operating and financial expenses but before dividend payments.

net free cash flow   Cash flow minus capital expenditures.

noise   Stock price changes that cannot be explained by changes in fundamentals.

overvalued   A stock for which the price is above the value range. Such a stock is a sell candidate.

payout ratio   Fraction of earnings paid out as dividends. Equals one minus the retention ratio.

PE   Price per share divided by earnings per share.

PS   Price per share divided by revenues per share.

relative PE   The company's PE divided by the industry-wide or market-wide PE.

ROE   Return on equity. Earnings divided by shareholder equity.

retention ratio   Fraction of earnings retained by the company. Equals 1 minus the payout ratio.

shareholder equity   Book value or net worth of the company, the accumulated money invested in the firm by shareholders. Comprised of paid-in-capital, retained earnings and net of treasury stock as well as other adjustments.

sustainable growth   The growth rate the firm can maintain without issuing new equity. Estimated as ROE times retention ratio.

TAT   Total assets turnover. Total revenues divided by total assets.

Timeliness   Short-term valuation of a stock estimated by *Value Line*. Number one's are the most timely over the next 12 months while number five's are the least timely.

VM   Value multiplier. The number used to scale a company characteristic such as EPS in order to estimate the fundamental value of the stock.

value range   The range of estimated fundamental values for the company.

undervalued   Stock for which the price is below the value range. Such a stock is a buy candidate.

Index

▼ ▼ ▼

About the Author
▼ ▼ ▼

C. Thomas Howard, Ph.D., is a professor of finance at the Daniels College of Business, University of Denver, and specializes in the area of investment management and international finance. He is Director of the MBA Program which has received national acclaim as being one of the most innovative in the country. In addition, Dr. Howard has been a guest lecturer at SDA Bocconi, Italy's leading business school, and at Handelshøjskole Syd in Denmark. He presents seminars throughout the United States for the American Association of Individual Investors, which is headquartered in Chicago, Illinois. He also has consulted with a number of firms, including *USWEST* and Cyprus Minerals.

Dr. Howard has published both articles and business cases dealing with a range of topics, including international finance, portfolio management and risk management. His work has appeared in academic journals as well as more popular publications such as *Barron's*. He is regularly quoted in the local as well as the national media and has made both TV and radio appearances.